WOULD YOU LIKE YOUR BOOK
TO BE ON THIS BESTSELLER LIST?

Leaves of Grass
Tarzan and the Apes
The Tale of Peter Rabbit
Bartlett's Quotations
Huckleberry Finn
Lady Chatterly's Lover
Ulysses
The First Whole Earth Catalog
The One-Minute Manager
Winning by Intimidation

All of the above books were originally published by their authors themselves. Today, in the age of the word processor, it is easier than ever to join them—with the information and resources provided by—

THE
SELF-PUBLISHING
HANDBOOK

DAVID M. BROWNSTONE and IRENE M. FRANCK are a husband-wife team with extensive experience in publishing, packaging, and writing. Their many previous books, singly and jointly, include *Where to Find Business Information, Personal Financial Survival, The Dictionary of Publishing,* and *The Historical Encyclopedia of Work.*

THE
SELF-PUBLISHING
HANDBOOK

— ☆ —

*David M. Brownstone
and Irene M. Franck*

A Hudson Group Book

A PLUME BOOK
NEW AMERICAN LIBRARY
NEW YORK AND SCARBOROUGH, ONTARIO

NAL BOOKS ARE AVAILABLE AT QUANTITY DISCOUNTS WHEN USED TO PROMOTE
PRODUCTS OR SERVICES. FOR INFORMATION PLEASE WRITE TO PREMIUM
MARKETING DIVISION, NEW AMERICAN LIBRARY, 1633 BROADWAY,
NEW YORK, NEW YORK 10019.

PLUME TRADEMARK REG. U.S. PAT. OFF. AND FOREIGN COUNTRIES
REGISTERED TRADEMARK—MARCA REGISTRADA
HECHO EN WESTFORD, MASS., U.S.A.

SIGNET, SIGNET CLASSIC, MENTOR, PLUME, MERIDIAN AND NAL BOOKS are
published *in the United States* by New American Library, 1633
Broadway, New York, New York 10019, *in Canada* by The New
American Library of Canada Limited, 81 Mack Avenue, Scarborough,
Ontario MIL 1M8

Library of Congress Cataloging in Publication Data

Brownstone, David M.
  The self-publishing handbook.

  "A Hudson Group book."
  Bibliography
  Includes index.
  1. Self-publishing—Handbooks, manuals, etc.
I. Franck, Irene M. II. Title.
Z285.5.B76   1985   070.5   84-20662
ISBN 0-452-25685-2

First Printing, April, 1985

1 2 3 4 5 6 7 8 9

PRINTED IN THE UNITED STATES OF AMERICA

Contents

Preface

Our intent in writing this *Self-Publishing Handbook* is to provide help for authors who are seriously considering publishing their works on their own—or have already decided to do so.

We have both been professionals in several branches of the publishing trade for many years, in the last decade moving over from publishing and editing into writing, so we can fairly claim to have developed wide and deep knowledge of every aspect of the publishing process.

Beyond that personal knowledge and experience, though, we have relied upon the shared resources of a large number of experienced publishing people in preparing this book. They are, in truth, far too many to name here, their joint contribution going back many years before this book was even conceived. With some trepidation, then, and knowing that we will inevitably omit significant contributors, we thank the following people for their invaluable assistance in writing this book:

First, our Hudson Group associates, for ten years of always fruitful discussion on every aspect of publishing. They are: Bryan Bunch, Courtlandt Canby, Gorton Carruth, Eugene Ehrlich, Gene Hawes, Lawrence Lorimer, Robert O'Brien, David Scott, Bruce Wetterau, and former member Stuart Berg Flexner.

Ken Burke, George Delury, Fran Fishelberg, Pamela Fitzgibbon, Katherine Schowalter, Robin Smith, and David Sobel were especially helpful on the production side of publishing. Dick Zeldin, Judy Wilson, Ed Knappman, Cynthia Kirk, Dick McCullough, Olga and George Wieser, and a host of other publishing professionals most graciously answered a wide range of miscellaneous questions while the book was in progress. We thank them all.

Not least, we must also thank Arnold Dolin and Hugh Rawson, our editors at New American Library, whose idea this book is; and also Donna Cullen and Barbara Arnay for their able assistance in preparing the book for production.

Finally, we thank our expert typists, Shirley Fenn, Nancy Fishelberg, and Mary Racette, who, as always, have done some final copyediting as they have prepared the manuscript.

In the end, of course, the book—with its strengths and weaknesses—is our own. We hope that self-publishers will find in it useful guidance and advice.

David M. Brownstone
Irene M. Franck
Chappaqua, New York

THE
SELF-PUBLISHING
HANDBOOK

☆

CHAPTER 1

☆

Why Self-Publishing?

Self-publishing is an old and honorable pursuit. Walt Whitman's *Leaves of Grass,* Edgar Rice Burroughs's *Tarzan of the Apes,* Henry George's *Progress and Poverty,* Beatrix Potter's *The Tale of Peter Rabbit,* Mary Baker Eddy's *Science and Health, Robert's Rules of Order,* Bartlett's *Quotations*—all these and many other internationally famous books were originally published by their authors. Self-publishing is a well-worn path, rather than a new and untried publishing mode. Most of the ways in which authors can move their books from desk to print to market have been successfully explored by authors for at least the last two centuries. Indeed, the tradition goes back to the earliest days of printing, when writers like Erasmus mounted horses to carry their manuscripts halfway across Europe to printers, shepherding their work through each stage of publication.

Over a century ago, Ralph Waldo Emerson, Henry Wadsworth Longfellow, and Washington Irving were exploring several varieties of self-publishing. Emerson took his manuscripts all the way to finished books, paying a commission to his publisher for sales made; in his case, the publisher functioned much as some wholesalers do today. Emerson also spent most of his adult life on the lecture circuit and wrote a great many articles for the periodicals of his day—all of which helped sell his books. On the other hand, Longfellow went through the publishing process only as far as finished plates, and leased the plates to his publishers. Washington Irving went all the way through the publishing process, producing and selling several of his books as a self-publisher, including the *Sketch Book* and his *The Knickerbocker History of New York*.

Some major authors have self-published all or most of their work. Walt Whitman, revered now, struggled for most of his life to put his work into print in self-published form. William Blake lived in poverty but managed to publish his own work. Samuel Clemens self-published his own *Huckleberry Finn* and then the works of many other authors, turning publisher as well as writer and lecturer.

Some of those who were primarily self-publishers were extraordinary commercial successes. Mary Baker Eddy's self-published work provided the basis for the Christian Science movement, for example, and has sold millions of copies. Edgar Rice Burroughs published most of his own body of work, at great profit.

Many authors—all the way from Byron, Carl Sandburg, and T. S. Eliot to Zane Grey—have self-published their early work. Many others have published their own work and have had their work, once in print, picked up by commercial publishers and widely distributed. This is quite a strong modern trend, as well as an historic one. That was the pattern for such modern best-selling books as *The One-Minute Manager, The Last Whole Earth Catalog, Mary Ellen's Helpful Hints,* and *Winning Through Intimidation.* It was also what happened to *Lady Chatterley's Lover, Ulysses, Robert's Rules of Order, The Tale of Peter Rabbit,* and *Progress and Poverty.* It happened to Tom Paine's *Common Sense,* too—only Paine had no adequate copyright protection in that early period, and his work was stolen by his printers.

It is clear that a great many authors have published their own work, often with considerable literary and commercial success. Indeed, it is all too tempting to stress those success stories, and thereby distort reality. For every Emerson, Whitman, and Sandburg, there are a hundred authors whose names we no longer remember. For every great commercial success—for every Zane Grey, Edgar Rice Burroughs, Bartlett, Robert, or Eddy—there are a hundred hopeful authors who wrote and published a book or two, and then moved on. No matter; writers will do their best to write, whatever the rewards. And success stories are warming; some of them can be enlightening, as well.

Self-publishing is not for everyone, nor is it equally suitable for all types of books. But changes in the relationships between authors and publishers, in the economics of publishing in general, and in the production technology available, all make self-publishing a strong alternative to traditional publishing for many authors today.

The Situation of Authors Today

This is a time of considerable change in the linked worlds of writing, publishing, and bookselling—and the pace of change accelerates. We live and write in a world in which mass audiences turn toward television and formula fiction, and away from more demanding—and more literate—work. Casually written, poorly edited, badly produced pop psychology and how-to books crowd serious nonfiction off bookstore shelves. Publishers, many of whom are in deep economic trouble, reach for the kinds of safe potential bestsellers that will keep them afloat and perhaps even modestly profitable; writers of good, serious work find it very difficult to secure publishers for that work.

That is all true; it has also been the standard lament of writers, unhappy publishers, and booksellers for many years now. We can continue to lament and wait for better times that may not come, or we can analyze our situation and see how to successfully publish and distribute our work in changed circumstances.

Several trends have a great deal to do with the situation of authors today. First, there is a continuing and very long-term weakness in the world economy, which will not improve soon and which greatly affects an already weak American publishing industry. The private and public money that is available in boom times would help writers, as would the enhanced book buying that comes when people have a good deal of discretionary money to spend. But boom times, like those of the 1960s, will not come again for quite some time. We can, at best, reasonably expect only some modest upturns and some frightening downturns around a stagnant center, coupled with increasing technological unemployment as robots and computers replace people. Many industries, including some sections of the publishing industry, will continue to be weak, and some will be very sick indeed.

This is a climate in which we can expect publishers, especially trade book publishers, to continue to be wary of committing considerable sums of investment money to new books from any but very "bankable" authors; even some very well-known authors will have difficulty in placing some of their proposed books. Investment money will be forthcoming, certainly, as it is now for some books thought to be relatively "sure" to show a profit, but we cannot expect much to be available for the publishing of good or non-standard books, especially by unknown authors.

A second trend affecting authors is the continuing move from print to screen forms, which began with the advent of the movies, accelerated greatly with the introduction of television, and is now accelerating once again as special-purpose television and computer-connected screens of several kinds begin to appear in homes and workplaces. It is likely that, in the long run, most of humanity will be reading print on screen and that books will thereby complete an historic transition from print to screen, with a far larger number of very literate readers—and very prosperous writers—than ever before. But in the short run—in this period—that mass move from print to screen means fewer readers for our books now, as book-reading habits fade and screen-watching habits grow.

Special-interest Markets

A third such trend is the fragmentation of general book markets into special-interest book markets. This has made it very difficult for many general trade publishers to reach for the natural prime audiences of many books through traditional bookstore sales outlets. Publishers reaching for narrow bookbuying audiences by mail, and able to charge prices high enough to justify the intrinsically high cost of mail solicitation, have done rather well; this is notably true of some professional and reference publishers. But those general trade publishers whose books are priced too low, or are too general for special-interest audiences, or whose mail-selling skills have not developed in the right directions—or all three, which is often the case—continue to rely mainly upon bookstores for hardcover and trade paperback book sales. That has meant reaching more and more for lowest-common-denominator mass audiences, while competing for limited bookstore display space with many other publishers. Here Gresham's Law has been proven as operative for books as it did for money: the bad books drive out the good.

We should not expect the overwhelming majority of commercial publishers to behave otherwise, by the way. A marketplace economy has its own imperatives; even those publishers who continue to care about publishing good books must spend most of their time acquiring books that will sell well and generate profit. This is clearly so for publishers that have become the subsidiaries of other companies; there the publishing executive who loses money is soon replaced by someone else. But it is so for independent commercial publishers as well, though independents can—and in some instances do—try very hard to continue to publish good books. Yet the independent publisher must also pay all the bills, carry high rates of interest on borrowed money, keep stock values up, and pay dividends to often impatient investors. In the long run, the need for profit is the same for all commercial publishers; the difference is that some independents need not seek to profit as much and as consistently as do publicly held or conglomerate-owned publishers.

In one sense, the fragmentation of book markets has been a bad thing for many authors in that it makes it more difficult to place many kinds of books with commercial publishers. On the other hand, this trend also brings with it opportunity. Much more on this later, but for now let us point out only that authors are not hindered by the same kinds of profit imperatives that commercial publishers face. Nor do authors have to pay for expensive office space or support substantial numbers of employees, some of them making a good deal more money than do most authors. An author will usually find it much harder to reach national markets with a general-audience book than will most commercial publishers. But a self-publisher will very often be able to reach local, regional, or narrow markets far less expensively and more profitably than will a commercial publisher. All of this means that an author may very often profit decently and sometimes even handsomely from a book that a commercial publisher would not and really should not be willing to publish at all. Putting it a little differently, a book that may be quite properly seen as a foolish gamble by a commercial publisher may be a perfectly sensible candidate for publication by its own author.

Production Economies

To a considerable extent, self publishing has become more attractive because of the development of a fourth major trend, which is in the economics of book composition and manufacturing. Self-publishing authors today face far more favorable composition and production costs than did authors in mid-century. The author who wanted to self-publish before the mid-1950s had to compose very expensively in hot metal type and then go on to produce hardcover books with printers whose equipment and attitudes made short-run printing very expensive indeed. A page of ordinary and straight-forward type might typically cost $12–$15 in hot metal, and much more if tabular setting were involved. A short run of hardcovered books might easily cost $5–$10 per book. And that was in thirty-years-ago dollars; $12–$15 per page in the mid-1950s translates into $35–$42 in the mid-1980s. Trade paperbacks were then just beginning to be published, and had little acceptance among book-buyers and librarians.

Even fifteen years ago, after the composition revolution that replaced hot metal type and metal printing plates with cold type and photographic processes, composition costs were much higher than they are today. A publisher fifteen years ago might have been pleased to buy a page of ordinary book type for $6–$10 and a short run of hardcovered books for $2–$4 per book. That translates in real dollars today roughly into $17–$28 per page for composition and $5–$11 per short-run book.

Today, self-publishing authors with word processors hitched to personal computers have extraordinarily inexpensive composition machines and may be able to produce composed pages for as little as $2 per page, even including something for their own time spent in typing corrections and coding the text into the desired format. That is, in real dollars, about 5 percent of what that page would have cost to set thirty years ago, and about 10 percent of the real-dollar cost fifteen years ago. Those composing with professional compositors may still pay $6–$10 per page, but that is, in real dollars, about 20 percent of the cost thirty years ago and 35 percent of the cost fifteen years ago.

Today's hardcover book is, for long runs, no more expensive than it was thirty and fifteen years ago, although new technology and manufacturing approaches make today's short run in real dollars somewhat less expensive. But today's short-run trade paperback is strikingly less expensive than yesterday's hardcover book—and that is the main real comparison for self-publishers. Today, the relatively short-run, modestly sized trade paperback, for which you can usually charge almost as much as a hardcover book, may cost as little as fifty cents to a dollar, as against $3–$8 for its hardcover equivalent. The widespread and growing acceptance of the trade paperback by libraries can, in many instances, even eliminate the need for hardcover library editions of books, for many librarians see trade paperbacks as something of a bargain as against most hardcovers.

Hardcover or soft, the economics of self-publishing have changed greatly, and much for the better. Small wonder, then, that self-publishing authors and small publishers are multiplying. The wonder, really, is that so few large trade publishers have found it possible to adapt their operations to the new and very favorable economics of small-scale publishing. Most large professional and reference publishers have long since done so.

Both word-processing technologies and full trade-paperback acceptance are very recent phenomena; together they greatly and wholly favorably change self-publishing economics.

Distribution Changes

In the 1970s and early 1980s we have also seen major changes in book distribution techniques and patterns, so important as to constitute a fifth major trend. For example, mail-order selling has become rather a big business, in books as throughout the economy. This has meant that both highly specific mailing lists and very skilled mailing houses have become readily available to self-publishing authors, as they have long been to large businesses. That makes it possible for authors to sell their books by mail directly to narrow specialist markets far more easily and profitably than ever before.

Along similar lines, substantial direct face-to-face bookselling opportunities have developed as authors read and speak to college audiences, conventions, meetings, and television audiences. The author who can link up normal speaking and teaching activities with self-publishing can and often does achieve excellent and highly profitable book sales.

This period has also seen the rapid growth of the chain bookstore and, with it, the possibility of thousands of book sales from a single chain placement. In addition, increasing numbers of independent book representatives are handling book sales for many publishers at a time. Both developments can be highly favorable to self-publishing authors if properly understood and worked with. We will have more, much more, on the opportunities stemming from new techniques and patterns of book distribution later on in this book.

A sixth major trend has been the development of a substantial body of skilled publishing freelancers, many of them capable of taking a manuscript all the way from early deep editing right on through production and sale of finished books. Given their presence and accessibility on the publishing scene, even the most timorous of authors need no longer see self-publishing as anything but a viable alternative to commercial publishing.

Publishing Difficulties

Beyond these major trends, several developments within the publishing industry itself have had adverse impact upon writers, causing them to consider the self-publishing alternative much more seriously than ever before.

Not so long ago, some of the best advice you could give a new writer was to find a good agent, preferably someone working in or very near the New York metropolitan area, who knew everybody in and everything about the very small and incestuous world of New York publishing. Once represented by that kind of agent, and assuming even basic writing and thinking competence on the writer's part, it would then be only a matter of time before your books began to be placed. That was quite true not so long ago—but not now. Today, even experienced and well-connected agents often find it difficult to place the work of many of their established clients, much less the work of newcomers. Oh, some do, of course; there are still real success stories to tell. But in this period it is very hard to find a well-established agent who will seriously take on newcomers; worse, it is very hard to place books with publishers even if you have an established agent.

If you do place a book, that book is more likely than before to be placed as a trade paperback—a paperback book marketed mainly through bookstores, but in size and content otherwise like the hardcover books around it. Except for the price. Trade paperbacks cost less than hardcover books, making them in these times attractive to many bookbuyers.

The problem for the author of a book published primarily in trade paper is that royalty rates—and therefore the advances against royalties offered by publishers—are much smaller than for equivalent hardcover books. The standard hardcover royalty is 10 percent of cover price for the first 5,000 copies sold, 12½ percent of cover price for the second 5,000 copies sold, and 15 percent of cover price thereafter. The standard trade paperback contract is 6 to 8 percent of cover price for the first 10,000–20,000 copies sold and 8 to 10 percent of cover price thereafter. Therefore, a hardcover book selling a total of 20,000 copies at $15 each is likely to yield approximately $39,000 in royalties.

Royalty income for $15 hardcover book:	
5,000 copies @ 10 percent royalty	$7,500
5,000 copies @ 12½ percent royalty	9,375
10,000 copies @ 15 percent royalty	22,500
	$39,375

However, a trade paperback edition of precisely the same book selling 20,000 copies at the probable price of $9.95 may yield as little as $12,000 and no more than $18,000. If you take the probable sale of the book down to 6,000 copies—a reasonable figure for many modestly selling works of both fiction and nonfiction—the hardcover royalties become what might be a modestly livable $9,400. But the trade paperback royalties become a very small $3,600–$4,800 for most authors. The royalty advance the publisher actually offers a writer will reflect the royalties expected to be earned by the book, for publishers will want to do books that "earn out" their royalty advances. All of this makes the economics of writing through trade paperback publishers rather grim for authors in this period.

Nor can book authors reasonably expect to "piece it out" through hard times with magazine articles, as might have been possible in the last generation. Magazine-writing markets are, if anything, in worse condition than book-writing markets, with article rates generally far lower in real dollars than at any time since the Great Depression.

Writers' unions can be helpful, especially when dealing with those publishers who see difficult times for writers as an opportunity to behave as abominably as they possibly can, without a shred of even ordinary business ethics. But writers' unions will not solve the deep and persistent problems besetting the general trade book industry, which publishes most of the kinds of books authors want to write.

The Self-Publishing Alternative

Given these problems, many authors in the coming period will want to seriously consider the self-publishing alternative, along with the possibility of publishing through very small publishers owned by others and through author's cooperatives. Our focus here will be on self-publishing, though much of the book will apply to the small publisher and cooperative alternatives as well.

We speak here of *self-publishing*. Becoming publisher of your own written work in book, mixed media, or nonbook form, means taking ultimate responsibility for the whole process of preparing, producing, selling, physically distributing, and collecting money for your work, as well as for all the business functions which inevitably relate to the funding of any business, however small. For make no mistake about this: the decision to publish your own work is a decision to undertake everything any other publisher might undertake in behalf of your work, within the context of running a small—sometimes a very small—business of your own. No matter how skilled the help you secure, the financial and publishing responsibilities are ultimately yours. And however you measure profit or loss, in dollars and intangibles, they are yours, too.

You may self-publish work that you have written alone or with a co-author, or work that is only in small part yours, as when you do an anthology or a handbook composed mainly of articles written by others. Should you publish your own work and then move into the publication of works written by others as well, then you will become both self-publisher and publisher. Should you stop publishing your own work and continue to publish the work of others, you will become a publisher, whatever work you continue to write for publication by others. These are not merely matters of definition, for they identify focus—and hazard.

For a writer, one of the key hazards connected with self-publishing is the possibility of becoming so fascinated with the process of publishing that you lose concentration upon writing. Publishing is fine if it is what you really want to do; but most writers write because they must, and a frustrated writer turned almost-full-time publisher is likely to be half-satisfied—and probably not much good at—either writing or publishing. For the dedicated writer, self-publishing is essentially a defensive set of moves, aimed at getting written work from desk to audience—and at making enough money to at least survive and be able to write on many other days. If a little commercial success as a publisher turns you away from your writing, then you have paid far too high a price for that little bit of success. But if, on the other hand, it allows you to keep on writing, then it is success indeed.

Self-Publishing Is Not Vanity Publishing

Let us distinguish here between taking the responsibility for publishing your own work, which is self-publishing; having your work published by a publishing house, which takes some risk in publishing that work; and paying a publisher to publish your work. This last alternative is sometimes mistaken for self-publishing by neophytes, but it is really an expensive blind alley: vanity publishing.

It is very easy to assume that if you are willing to spend time and money writing and publishing your own book, it is essentially the same thing and perhaps much more efficient to just write the book and pay an experienced publisher to worry about producing and marketing it. After all, many small publishers—and a startling number of large ones—pay little or nothing in the way of advances against royalties, and you know nothing at all about publishing. The publisher who so obligingly advertises for authors in the book review or writer's magazine you read wants only a few thousand dollars to do it all—and, of course, disarmingly supplies proof stories about how so many have made money by taking this very easy path to publication.

Well, it would all make sense if vanity publishers actually produced all the books they imply they will produce; if they really sold books hard, instead of relying upon the payments of authors for their profits; and if most people in the book trade did not consider vanity press imprints upon books to be the kiss of death. But if all those things were true, vanity presses would be reputable publishers rather than traps for unwary, hopeful, rather bemused authors.

A vanity press is a publisher that advertises for and otherwise seeks out authors, contracts to publish their books, and charges them some thousands of dollars for having those books published. Vanity presses normally produce a few books, holding the rest of the promised press run in sheets rather than in bound books. They advertise minimally, usually with group advertisements for many books in a few book reviews or other periodicals, and do not really expect to sell many copies of your book. They are quite happy when a book sells decently, almost always due to its author's promotional efforts, but will do nothing much to help it sell, as their essential business is to make profit from the author's payments to them. Their promised editing assistance usually turns out to be a very minimal copyediting job, with good, bad, and simply awful work all treated equally and made into books. Most vanity publishers successfully protect themselves against charges of actionable fraud with very carefully constructed disclaimers and author-publisher contracts. (Vanity publishing is sometimes mislabeled subsidy publishing, which is quite different, being the publishing of works supported by institutional grants of several kinds.)

For those few authors who want only to see their work in print, who care little or nothing about money, and who are unwilling to take even the most elementary steps toward self-publication, a vanity press publication may make sense. But such authors are few and far between. Most authors who turn to vanity presses do not know what they are getting into, and have no idea that there are entirely feasible and less expensive solutions that are far more acceptable out in the publishing marketplace. Even aside from the cost, trying to sell your book with a vanity press imprint on it is like pushing a huge stone uphill. If you have any doubt at all about that, go into several reputable bookstores in your community, with the names of some of the presses that advertise for authors, and look for the books of those publishers on the store shelves. If you feel the need to go further, go to the public library and search for the books of those publishers on the library's shelves. If you see one, turn to the first leaf of the book, and you are quite likely to see that it was donated to the library by its author or a member of the author's family. The truth is that bookstores seldom stock and libraries seldom buy vanity press books; they have a bad reputation among booksellers and librarians.

If you are a neophyte and have some money you are willing and able to spend on your book, almost any publishing mode is better than going to a vanity press. It is far better, for instance, to hire a competent freelance editor, who may cut your book up one side and down the other, in the process helping you create a book you can really be proud of. Then you can learn something about self-publishing and publish it yourself, or find a small or large publisher that is willing to put some time and money into producing and selling your work. Either way you will still probably get little or no advance against royalties, and you will still invest some money in making the book fit for publication and then publishing and marketing it; but you will have written and published a real book, with your self-respect intact and with a real chance for recognition and even for some commercial success in the book marketplace. You would have no such chance with a vanity publisher.

For many authors, self-publishing is, from the start, at least as good a way to go as commercial publishing. For others, the choice can go either way, with resolution depending upon capital and skills. And for others, especially many of those for whom going the standard commercial publishing way has been taken for granted, self-publishing may provide control, flexibility, and the ability to make far more money than their work has so far yielded.

Successful self-publishing requires some learning, though. To self-publish, you must know something about the publishing process, how to handle the main specifics of editing, manuscript preparation, composition, manufacture, book costing, pricing, mailing, selling, promotion—and a little bit about how to start and run a small business, too. It sounds like a lot, doesn't it? Well, reflect on the fact that young people just a few years out of college and with no previous publishing, editing, or marketing training occupy many key jobs in American publishing and bookselling today, and take another look at yourself and your capabilities. There is no reason at all for a writer to back away from self-publishing because of imagined lack of aptitudes and training. With sufficient motivation and patient attention, any writer can learn how to publish his or her own work, and do it well. That makes an overview of the publishing process the next order of business, and the next chapter of this book.

CHAPTER 2

———————— ☆ ————————

What You Need To Know About The Publishing Process

If you want to publish one book or a hundred books, your own book or the books of others, you must know a good deal about the several intertwined and interdependent processes involved in bringing a book before its audiences, as well as something of the business side of publishing. No, you need not be able to run Random House or McGraw-Hill to self-publish your own work; but the essential publishing and business processes are quite the same, whether your book is self-published or brought out by a large commercial publisher. They differ only in such subsidiary matters as the sequencing of some events, in financing arrangements, and, usually, in scale. Here is an outline of the publishing process, function by major function, aimed at providing an overview of the entire process. (A flow chart showing the process is also provided in Appendix 2). We will discuss each function and the choices surrounding it in more detail later on in this book.

Writing and Editing

First, you have to write the book. When you do a book with a commercial publisher, you may submit a proposal, with an outline and perhaps some sample material, get a contract and an advance against royalties, and settle down to write the book. While you are writing—and especially once you have a good idea as to when you will complete the book—your publisher will be developing promotion and marketing plans, and may be seriously engaged in attempting to sell book club, paperback, foreign, serialization, and other subsidiary rights many months before you even finish. But when you self-publish, you must write the book first, because until you have something very substantial to show—at least bound galleys of your completed manuscript—you are unlikely to be able to do any serious marketing, promotion, or subsidiary rights selling. This difference in the sequencing of selling activities could add up to a significant set of disadvantages for self-publishers—except that only a few commercially published books get the kind of pre-publication attention described above, and those are increasingly the "blockbusters" that commercial publishers feel obliged to seek from celebrities and "bankable" authors.

So first the book itself, from idea through the creation of your completed manuscript, and with as little diversion from the writing process as possible. For most of us, concentration is very close to all while writing a book; to the many potentially jarring distractions outside our control, it is unwise to add a too-early concentration on publishing plans and mechanics. Remember that a book can take far longer to write than you had supposed, and that too-early contacts may have to be re-established and plans redone if you finish your book considerably later than you had planned. Freelancers can become unavailable; printers may move or change price schedules; and your own plans may change a great deal during the months or years in which you are creating a book. For self-publishers, then, a cardinal rule: first write the book.

Only if you have published with others or have self-published previous books should you be deeply involved in the publishing process while writing, and then only as a matter of necessity. And when writing a book, do your best to set aside as many large blocks of prime time as possible, minimizing other potentially distracting involvements during those periods. You may be able to turn out sound work while you are tired and distracted; if many writers couldn't do that, far fewer books would be written. But if you can do good work when you are not at your best, consider how much better your work can be if you are fresh and fully focused for long enough periods that allow you to get deep into the work.

To write the book before seriously starting to publish and sell it is not to ignore its marketplace possibilities. Whether by choice or simply in fact, you are likely to be writing for audiences that can be defined, and that definition supplies the context within which all publishing decisions will be made, including production and marketing decisions and expenditures.

Although this book is about publishing rather than writing, one very important publishing function straddles both fields and is of great importance for the writer—especially for neophytes. That is the developmental editing function. A developmental editor—preferably an experienced editor other than the author—acts as a guide and sounding board, giving professional advice on the development of the work in its early stages. Securing competent developmental editing help early in the writing process can be vitally important, whether you are self-publishing or publishing through others. Indeed, this key element of publishing is fast disappearing from commercial houses and must more and more be supplied by authors themselves.

Whether you work with a developmental editor early on or not, creation of a piece of work—of any length, in any form—requires writing, rewriting, editing, and rewriting again, as necessary. If your book has illustrations, it may also require the creation of maps, drawings, charts, graphs, photographs, and other illustrative material. In the course of preparing your manuscript. you may work with such people as artists, mapmakers, and photo researchers, who may produce, research, or secure such illustrations. You may also need to secure permissions to quote or otherwise draw material from other copyrighted works, possibly using an experienced editor to help you.

Ultimately, on your own or with the help of various experienced people, you will have created and refined a final manuscript. At that point, having finally set the order and content of the materials in your book, you will be able to also create a final title page; a preface, foreword, and introduction, if any or all of these are desired; a table of contents; and any other desired items of front or back matter. Some nonfiction authors also then begin to go through their manuscripts to prepare word and subject lists for their indexes, but in our view that is premature. You will most efficiently prepare an index only when you have a final set of numbered page proofs before you, and that is still several steps away.

Now you will move into the copyediting of your finished manuscript. In a few rare and special situations, you may choose to do all editing functions yourself; that choice may be entirely valid if you are publishing poetry, for example. But in almost every other instance, editing your own work is an elementary and probably disastrous error; it is a job for a professional other than yourself. If you have worked with an editor to develop the manuscript, then whoever copyedits your final manuscript may do simple copyediting—checking and correcting spelling, consistency, grammar, and related matters, and marking the text for composition. But if you have not worked with a developmental editor, a copyeditor coming to your unedited manuscript may, at your request, do anything from a very deep editing of your work—which might involve radical revision and your subsequent rewrite—to a light cosmetic job to make the work superficially correct, with no glaring spelling or grammatical errors. In any case, you as author will go back and forth with the copyeditor until the manuscript has again been finished, this time ready for composition into book pages.

Composition and Production

In this period, you will also be designing, costing, and pricing the book, and developing specifications for such matters as type, paper, bindings, and colors to be followed by the book's compositor and then manufacturer. You will also be preparing a design and writing selling copy for the cover, whether you are going to be publishing a hardcover book with a separate dust jacket or a paperback with copy on its front and back covers. In dealing with these complicated matters, you will profit greatly by working with a competent book designer, whether a freelancer you employ or a designer associated with the firm that manufactures your books. As with editing, you may do it all yourself, but the results are usually very disappointing.

If you are using a computerized word-processing system, you may have designed some elements of your book much earlier; you may actually have been doing the composition of the book as you or your typist typed your words into the computer, then coded it for your desired format. But whether you use conventional methods or the newer computerized word-processing technology, and whether you hire expert help or do it yourself, these editing and design functions must be performed if the final result is to be a professional-looking book.

Using conventional methods, your copyedited manuscript will now go to composition. Using a word processor, your now copyedited and coded manuscript will be in your computer's memory, probably on one or more discs; it may even be ready to produce camera-ready copy—that is, copy from which plates can be made which are used in printing machines. Either way, on screen or on paper, you as author will now read the book in print, either directly in page form or first in the form of galleys, which are columns not yet made up into pages. At this stage, you will make any final changes or corrections, reading your work both for meaning and for typographical errors. You may also employ a proofreader at this stage, as it is very hard indeed even for professional writers to see typographical errors in their own work. After corrections are made, the manuscript is made up into pages and paginated, or numbered. With page numbers in place, you can prepare an index if your book is to contain one.

Then, unless you are yourself a professional or hobbyist printer, you will hire someone to print and bind your book. We here use "book" in the widest sense, for your "book" may be anything from a small, self-covered, unstitched typewriter-composed pamphlet to a large, hardbound, heavily illustrated artbook or multi-volume work. It may be a set of unbound pages set into a looseleaf binder or, for that matter, a set of cards in a box. In the not very distant future, some books may not be print on paper at all, but rather works carried in computer memories, capable of being viewed on screen or as printouts.

The result is your book—many books, as many as you have had printed and bound. (You may also have some sheets, run at the same time, but not bound until later, if and when needed.) You will have done some necessary formal things along the way, such as securing an ISBN (International Standard Book Number) number for your book. Now, with book in hand, you will make a copyright registration.

Marketing and Business Handling

Although a book in a warehouse or basement has been published, the publishing process is still far from complete. Now your book has to be taken to its audiences. So far, all has been outgo for the author-publisher; now it is time to recoup cash expenditures, get some return for time expended, and perhaps some profit besides, to serve as capital for the development of other self-published books.

For author-publishers, real marketing should start between the time the manuscript is finished and the production of finished books, while the book is being copyedited, composed, and manufactured. Earlier, you run the twin risks of distraction and premature promotion that wastes time, money, and contacts; later—after production—it may be too late to make any serious approach to some potentially very valuable pre-publication review media and subsidiary rights sales possibilities. Earlier, as the book is being written, you may be revising themes and content, and therefore audience appeal. Now, with manuscript in hand, you are able to think about your audiences very clearly and to develop promotional approaches and materials aimed directly at them.

Before publication, self-publishers, like commercial publishers, should try to produce sets of softbound galleys or page proofs to be sent to several reviewers, who will only review copies received before publication; pre-publication timing is important, because they review primarily for the book trade, which relies to some extent on their evaluation in stocking forthcoming books for sale to the trade and to the public. Pre-publication bound galleys should also go to several other reviewers and to those book clubs that might be interested in buying your book.

While their books are being composed and manufactured, self-publishers should also be preparing press releases and advertising copy, and securing lists of those to whom review copies and press releases will be sent. Although commercial publishers, selling a whole list of books, often place advertisements well in advance of the publication of their spring and autumn "lines," an author self-publishing a single book is wise to prepare ads, but not place them until the book is physically in hand. Many things can happen to a book during production, and to spend advertising money selling a book that nobody yet has for sale is a waste of often irreplaceable marketing money.

Once the book is successfully off the press, there are many things to do. Review copies must be sent from a small supply you have had rushed from the printer; such copies should go out to reviewers within days of manufacture.

There are press releases to be sent, announcing the book; advertisements to be placed; bookstores and chains of bookstores to see and sell; distributors to talk with; libraries to sell; special lists to rent for selling by mail, if appropriate; interviews to arrange; meetings and conventions at which to speak, exhibit, and sell; and the costs of all such activities to firmly grasp and evaluate. A little later, there may be agents to see and commercial publishers to talk to. In short, with book in hand, you are going to announce publication to the world and move as actively and successfully as you can to bring your book and its audiences together.

Part of the publishing process has to do with the physical and financial handling of the books themselves. Where and how to store your books, how to bill, how to collect, how to handle the inevitable returns from booksellers, how to mail and in what packages—all these and more must be settled, as cost-efficiently as possible.

Throughout the whole publishing process, for author-publishers and commercial publishers alike, run the multiple and related questions of cost, price, credit, and capital. For authors, the most basic difference of all between publishing through a commercial publisher and self-publishing is that, in addition to writing the book, the author-publisher is also generating and financing a business enterprise, however small. That makes it necessary for the self-publisher to function as a small business owner as well as author. And, like every small business owner, the author-publisher must therefore understand and handle money and business questions every step of the way. For many, the self-publishing experience is an unexpectedly large and damaging financial and emotional drain. For others, it is a source of profit and personal satisfaction. The difference in personal reactions and situations often stems from differences in original choice of content, and therefore intrinsically different profit possibilities. More often, though, it is a matter of having thought through choices and developed cost-effective publishing approaches. The self-publishing author who thinks hard about money and watches every penny is not a sterile pennypincher. Far from it. That author is much more likely to be someone who has decided to become good enough at publishing to publish well now—and to do so again and again over the years if desired. Now, then, we turn to the vitally important money and business side of self-publishing.

CHAPTER 3

☆

Choices, Costs, and Prices

The kind of book you want to do, your ability to directly and inexpensively reach potential audiences for that book, and the kind of financial investment you are willing and able to put into the book—all of these things deeply affect your self-publishing decisions.

One of the safest and most logical candidates for self-publishing is the book you write as an expert with direct access to your natural audiences. For example, the professional who spends much time each year speaking to lay and professional audiences at conventions, association meetings, seminars, and college courses, is constantly facing an existing set of audiences for one or more books. Such books are likely to be very easy to write, stemming as they do from day-to-day work in the field and often being little more than a reworking of spoken materials, probably with some amplification.

They can be relatively easy and inexpensive to produce, as well, when you are selling directly to such audiences. Yours is the only book before them at the point of sale, and it will sell to them just as well in an inexpensively designed and produced paperback as it will in hardcover and on glossy paper. You can also sell the book through ads placed in special-interest publications, especially if you are a known figure in your field. While such books can also often be placed in local bookstores, direct sales to ready customers are both easier and more profitable.

Experts' books like these often make far more money for their authors when self-published than they do when placed with commercial publishers. Consider some numbers: A commercially published trade paperback will, in this period, normally yield a royalty rate of 6 percent of cover price for the first 10,000–20,000 copies sold and 7 to 8 percent of cover price thereafter. Should the expert's book be priced at $12.95 and sell 10,000 copies—and that is a reasonable kind of possibility for such special-interest trade paperbacks—royalties will come to 6 percent of $129,500, for a total of $7,770.

Assume that the same book, self-published at the same $12.95 price, yields only 5,000 sales, half the sales achieved by the commercial publisher. Let us say that average revenues per book to the self-publisher come to 90 percent of cover price, because the overwhelming majority of sales come as direct full-price sales to live audiences. Your self-publishing gross revenue is then $58,275. Take from that sum the cash expenditures you have made as a self-publisher. In this instance, assume they are: $2,000 for organization and overhead costs; $2,500 for composition; $7,500 for manufacturing 5,000 smallish, inexpensively produced books; $3,000 for the quite minimal advertising and promotion costs incurred for this kind of directly sold book; $1,000 for the modest shipping costs involved, as you normally take quantities of the book with you to your audiences; $1,000 more for such miscellaneous expenses as telephones, gasoline, and the like; and $2,000 more for some minimal freelance help secured along the way, mostly in copyediting and design advice. That all comes to $19,000. The figures may be a little high, as we have taken estimates from the upper part of the cost range. Now add 14 percent, or $2,660, to that $19,000, representing a combination of money that you could have been earning with the savings you used and of money actually paid in interest on the borrowings you made to finance the project. Total expenses therefore come to $21,660.

Subtracted from total income of $58,275, that leaves you with $36,615 for the time you have spent writing and promoting the book. You spent very little *extra* time promoting the book, by the way, as you took it directly to most of its buyers as part of your existing work. But, to be scrupulously fair in our comparison, let us assume that you spent 100 extra hours promoting the book, at $30 per hour, for a total of $3,000 in promotion time. That still leaves you $33,615 for writing the book, in contrast with the $7,770 you would have made had you sold twice as many with a commercial publisher. (Table 1 summarizes these figures.) That is close to

Table 1:
Author's Income:

Commercial Publication vs. Self-Publishing When Most Books
Are Sold Directly by Author-Publisher

Income from Self-Publishing
Revenue
5,000 books @ $12.95 ea. @ 90 percent discount $58,275

Expenses		
Organization & overhead	$ 2,000	
Composition	2,500	
Manufacturing	7,500	
Advertising & promotion	3,000	
Shipping	1,000	
Miscellaneous expenses (telephone, gas)	1,000	
Freelance help	2,000	
Foregone earnings	2,660	
Promotion time	3,000	
	$24,660	–24,660

Balance for Author $33,615

Income from Commercial Publishing
Royalty income
10,000 books (twice as many as above)
@ $12.95 ea. @ 6 percent (royalty) $ 7,770   – 7,770

Difference for Author $25,845

five times as much—and the comparison favors the self-publishing
decision more and more as you increase your sales.

In this instance, the key to success lies in the original decision
to self-publish in an area in which you have expert knowledge and
a set of captive audiences. Under these conditions, your promotion costs are very low, your fulfillment costs small, your uncol-
lectibles almost non-existent, and your revenue per book very high.
And you need not spend much per book on production to help con-
vince your audience to buy.

In these circumstances, it makes very little sense to go to a commercial publisher. To earn $32,000 with a commercial publisher, your book would have to sell close to 40,000 copies—and you are far more certain to sell 5,000 copies through personal efforts than a commercial publisher is likely to sell 40,000.

Going Commercial

On the other hand, it is usually possible for lecturing self-publishers to have the best of both the self-publishing and commercial publishing worlds. Should you want to move your work out to wide national markets after selling some thousands of copies in self-published form, you will have little difficulty in finding a willing commercial publisher. For then you and your book have a much coveted "track record," which can get you better royalty terms and a much larger promotional commitment to the book than you might have received initially.

Similarly, a screen lecturer, such as a cooking instructor with a local commercial or cable television show, is in an excellent position to do some self-publishing. The position is slightly different, but similarly advantaged. Here there are two quite substantial ways to sell books—one direct-to-audience and one through book outlets.

In the first instance, you can sell books directly off the screen; orders are sent to a box number and directly fulfilled at full price. At the same time, it is possible, with continuing media exposure, to get store placement throughout the viewing area, however large, and to sell many books through conventional bookselling channels. You will then need to sell to booksellers and perhaps jobbers at 40 to 50 percent off list price; you will also have some shipping costs for both direct and book outlet sales as well as billing and bad debt expenses for book outlet sales. But you may be able to sell many thousands of copies each way, even in a limited regional area, possibly providing the basis for later very substantial national sales. Your profit per book on direct sales will be much higher than your royalty would have been from a commercial publisher, even with shipping costs (and possibly a small sales percentage to the television station). Your profit per book on book outlet sales will be less than on direct sales, but will still be considerably higher than the royalties you would have been paid by a commercial publisher.

Poetry, Plays, and Novels

On a much smaller scale, but similarly situated, is poetry. No, you cannot expect to make any significant amount of money by selling your self-published poetry, but about the only way most poets are going to see substantial numbers of their poems in print is to publish those poems themselves. The economies of book publishing make it very difficult to publish the poems of even relatively well-known poets with more than a slim chance of achieving breakeven; that is why so few poets are published by commercial publishers.

But poets should and will publish their own work, and should be prepared to initiate readings—solo, or with other poets—at which they read and sell their work directly to as much of their audience as they can reach. If you compose and produce your poems modestly and in small press runs, and do not go to the expense of organizing yourself into a corporate business, you may get back all out-of-pocket cash costs and something besides, from direct sales at readings and personal placements at local and regional bookstores.

The key thing for self-publishing poets is to watch costs. You may find your work becoming popular over the years, as you become better known and perhaps strike popular themes and styles; but you had best not spend whatever money you have on trying to make that come true with expensive book production and marketing efforts. The odds are that you will get little bookstore placement outside your home area and that even there you will not sell many books in bookstores. You cannot expect to get national spread through normal chain, distributor, independent representative, and independent bookstore channels, either, for poetry is hard to make money on, and the small bookstore space allotted to poetry is usually taken up by the works of those established poets published commercially. Careful, inexpensive self-publishing is the answer, coupled with personal direct selling efforts and growing audience acceptance.

Some kinds of works are extraordinarily difficult to publish and sell at all effectively for either self-publishers or commercial publishers. Plays and screenplays, for example, have no market to speak of until they are produced, except that some plays, especially one-act plays, are picked up by specialty commercial publishers seeking work suitable for student and community theater productions. To self-publish and hope to sell a play or screenplay is rather unrealistic.

Some other kinds of works commonly published by commercial houses are difficult to self-publish with any real hope of profit and offer only a very slim hope of breakeven. Most novels, for example, are best published through others if at all possible. Even if you have a hard time finding a standard commercial publisher for your novel, you may be able to find a small press publisher who is willing to take something of a chance on your work. Most small press publishers are directly accessible through The International Association of Independent Publishers, listed in our Sources of Information section. If you do find it necessary to publish your novel yourself, however, consider joining or helping to initiate an authors' cooperative; you can develop more marketing strength together than anyone has alone. Do not misunderstand: you can certainly publish your own novel and make a serious effort to get pre-publication reviews in the book trade press and post-publication reviews in many other publications. If some key pre- and post-publication reviews are favorable, you may be able to get some distribution and both bookstore and library sales. It is just that this particular deck is stacked against the self-publisher with a single book in the marketplace rather than a "line" of books to sell or established distribution relationships. You may sell some thousands of copies of your novel, but the odds are that you will not and that your sales will be measured in the hundreds. Even if you place the book decently in bookstores, they may not sell well, with the bookstores eventually sending your unsalable novel back to you.

Even so, self-publishing is greatly preferable to publishing through a vanity publisher. Remember this: when a vanity publisher seems to be able to publish less expensively than you would be able to publish yourself, that is not a matter of greater publishing expertise and economy of scale. The difference is that you will spend time and money to seriously promote your book, and the vanity publisher will not. If you shop about a bit, and seek competent professional advice, you will always be able to produce your book less expensively and with much more long-term personal satisfaction than had you gone with a vanity publisher.

For the same basic marketing reasons, some other kinds of books also lend themselves better to publishing by others or to cooperative publishing than they do self-publishing. In general, authors have difficulty successfully selling their own nonfiction works in such areas as autobiography and biography, history, literature and literary criticism, philosophy, political science and international affairs, and the theatre and film arts. A book on a general subject of current topical interest has a somewhat better chance, but even then your self-published book will be competing for review and bookstore shelf space with many other books on the same "hot" subject, published by commercial houses with marketing strength.

Criteria for Self-Publishing

But non-fiction works can be prime candidates for self-publishing in certain circumstances. As we have discussed, authors who routinely reach people through lectures in person or on the screen are among the self-publishers most likely to succeed. The same is true of special-interest works—especially academic, professional, or reference books—that can successfully be sold through narrowly targeted direct-mail and advertising-placement efforts.

Let us take, for example, a specialist academic book. Given the politics of American higher education, many college teachers will still have to seek recognized academic and commercial publishers for their early work—to "publish so that they will not perish." And given the economics and marketing necessities of the textbook side of the book trade, academics will continue to need commercial publishers for textbooks. (Though many textbooks started out as photocopied manuscripts developed by a professor for classroom use and then picked up for wider distribution.) But an established academic who no longer has career reasons for publishing with a well-known commercial house should seriously consider the self-publishing alternative. If you are going to publish a relatively short work, with no tremendously expensive composition necessities, for a limited, well-defined audience, then examine the possibility of selling copies of the work directly to your own colleagues and specialist libraries around the country and world-wide. You may sell nearly the same number of copies as a commercial publisher and make some money doing it. That is especially likely if you can join others in your field in a cooperative publishing effort. One thousand copies of a $30 book sold direct or at a library discount through standard jobbers should yield you average revenue of perhaps $25 per book, or $25,000 in all. Your total costs, with all but your own time figured in, should be around $12,000–$15,000. The remaining $10,000–$13,000 for your time contrasts with the approximately $2,500 you would earn from the same 1,000 sales with an academic publisher. (Standard academic publishers' contracts pay 10 percent of publisher's net for the first 5,000 sales; 1,000 sales at a net of $25 each yields $25,000 net, of which 10 percent, or $2,500, would go to you.) And bear in mind that your advance with such a publisher is likely to range from nothing at all to perhaps $2,000, so you would have foregone very little in the way of advances against royalties.

A regional or local focus can also give a book special possibilities for self-publishing, especially when it is also on a subject of considerable current interest. A general work dealing with several major aspects of the American westward expansion throughout the nineteenth century may be personally satisfying, but terribly hard to sell to a national or international audience, no matter how well and astutely written. But a history of pioneer women in the northwest may sell thousands of copies in Oregon, Washington, and parts of several other states—and may have a chance at national distribution later if it does well selling regionally. From a marketing point of view, the key is to match content with the market you are yourself able to reach. An active author-publisher in the northwest, for example, is likely to be able to get excellent review attention, place books in bookstores, get regional distributor's help if desired, and in sum sell a regional book as well as or better than a national or regional commercial publisher might have done.

Similarly, a general travel book, cookbook, or sports book may be a difficult uphill push in the marketplace; but when done as a regional or even a very local book, it may do very well indeed. It is not only that marketing is easier in a smaller area, by the way; regional pride and interest can enhance the reader appeal of such books enormously.

Special-interest books are, by virtue of their content and definable markets, usually much easier for self-publishers—for that matter, for most publishers—to take to market. From a cultural point of view, it may be seen as unfortunate, but a lot more people continue to be interested in such mundane matters as money, sex, power, and business than in matters of high culture, and their book buying habits show it. If you do decide to self-publish a general book, be aware that—to sell it successfully to national markets—you may have to spend a good deal more in marketing the book than you did in writing and producing it. The numbers and risks change very much then; unless you are already expert in book marketing, you will be wise to seek out and listen hard to experts in this area. Even if you decide to "bootstrap" your book in terms of marketing expenditures, you will probably have to spend a good deal of marketing money even in the early stages—unless, of course, you have an existing low-cost or no-cost marketing vehicle, such as a television show or an ongoing national seminar series.

So far, we have assumed that your primary aim in writing a book is the creation of the book itself. However, that is not always so. Many authors view the book also as a means of making money, and perhaps of finding some measure of celebrity as well; for some, money and perhaps celebrity are even primary goals. If that is true for you, you might consider achieving some celebrity—and therefore marketability—even before you do your book. The lecture platform and the television screen first; then the book, perhaps first accompanying your other work and later standing alone. But if you do want to use the book itself as a path to money and celebrity, then you must be prepared to spend a good deal of marketing money to make money and build celebrity—and that will be high-risk money.

As we have seen, choice of form has much to do with kind of book, your ability to reach your natural markets, and your available investment money. But choice of form has other ramifications, as well. The first and most important of these has to do with the question of whether to publish your book in hardcover or in paperback.

Hardcover or Paperback

Hardcover books cost a good deal more to produce than trade paperbacks; the difference in costs is particularly large in the kinds of short runs that characterize most self-published books. And you generally cannot charge high enough prices for hardcover books to offset the increased costs. In purely economic terms, self-published trade paperbacks tend to be less expensive to produce and yield a higher profit percentage per unit than do hardcover books. However, other factors may be so important to self-publishers that they will make an otherwise uneconomic decision and publish in hardcover.

First, and most important, hardcovers get considerably more review attention than do paperbacks. Many books in both forms go substantially unreviewed, but a far higher proportion of hardcovers are reviewed than paperbacks. Even though paperbacks are coming to be more and more accepted by people in the world of books and bookselling, hardcovers still have much greater prestige than paperbacks, which translates into much more review attention.

That review attention can be make or break for some kinds of general self-published books. Favorable pre-publication reviews in *Publishers Weekly* and two or three other trade periodicals can mean substantial bookstore placements all over the country, which might not otherwise be available. Favorable post-publication reviews in *Library Journal* and two or three other library periodicals can make the difference between several thousand library sales and hardly any library sales at all. Librarians pay a great deal of attention to their own review media and to the specific recommendations made by reviewers in those periodicals.

Favorable reviews can also bring with them personal prestige; that can be enormously gratifying personally, no small matter for many authors. But they can also make it far easier to take your book to a commercial publisher after you have sold it successfully in the field as a self-published book—and to secure a contract with such a publisher for your next book, and the book after that if you wish. Good reviews will also help you secure competent agents, make book club sales, sell foreign rights, and do all the other things that come with having a commercially successful hardcover book.

Hardcover books are also still more acceptable to most librarians than paperbacks, even though paperbacks are more widely accepted for library use than ever before. That is a matter of simply utility. No matter how well-constructed, a paperback will be destroyed by heavy use far more quickly than a hardcover. The paper cover will curl with use and varying degrees of humidity; the flat back of the spine will break; the pages glued to the cover at the spine of the book will come loose. Although the more expensive trade paperbacks are more sturdily built than ever before, they still do not last nearly as well as standard hardcover books.

Hardcovers also work better for the reader. You can lay a well-used, well-built hardcover book flat on a table or other surface, and it will stay open in reading position. To accomplish that simple task with the overwhelming majority of trade paperbacks, you must first effectively break the back of the book—which also dramatically shortens its life.

That takes us to a prime, wholly uneconomic reason for some authors to publish their own works in hardcover, rather than paperback, if they can. If you have written the kind of book you want people to use for a long time—if you want some youngster fifty years on to walk into a library somewhere, pick up your book, use it, love it, and be made larger from having entered into a dialogue with you, then you will want to publish your work in durable form if at all possible.

The reverse, however, is not entirely true. Even if your book is intrinsically ephemeral—that is, composed of material that dates quickly and must periodically be updated and replaced—it does not always make sense to publish it in paperback only. Some directories, yearbooks, and tax and business books, for example, may work better in the marketplace in hardcover—or in hardcover and softcover editions for different markets. You may be able to charge more for a large directory in hardcover than you would have been able to charge in paperback. If you are selling to an affluent business or scientific market that buys such books primarily by mail, the economics of the book may work out better if you publish it wholly in hardcover. Or you may have a rather ephemeral book that is to be sold to both libraries and people buying in bookstores. The economics of that book may indicate two editions:

a hardcover library edition and a paperback edition for regular bookstore and other trade distribution channels.

Your basic decision is whether to publish in hardcover, softcover, or both. The esthetic, functional, and economic choices that affect your decision will also affect your choices of paper, print, binding quality, and several design elements. More on these choices in later chapters, which deal with the specifics of moving from manuscript through camera-ready copy to finished books.

Costs

It is the business side of publishing that is most daunting to the vast majority of potential self-publishers. For all but those few authors with publishing or general business backgrounds, publishing as a business is *terra incognita,* full of pitfalls, each of which is perfectly capable of swallowing up the modest resources of an author turned publisher.

That can be true—but need not be so at all for those authors who recognize that publishing one or more books is, in its financial and business essentials, no different from going into any other small business. Then business imperatives take over on the publishing side; the book you have labored to write as artist-creator becomes, for all practical purposes, a commodity to be produced cost-effectively, costed out carefully, priced correctly, promoted and sold well, and distributed efficiently. It is also a source of profits which can be used for business-building purposes—as in the creation and publication of more books—or for other personal purposes.

As with any business, you must understand your costs. In self-publishing, the first and often the largest of the main costs involved is the time you spend writing your book. When you write a book with an advance against future royalties from a commercial publisher, some revenue, no matter how small, results from your writing of the book. When you self-publish, you write the whole book on speculation—with high hopes and great plans, but on speculation nevertheless. You may publish the book, make a valiant effort to sell it, and—to put it inelegantly and sharply—fall flat on your face. Indeed, if your book is a thinly disguised autobiographical novel, a tract on the evils of the day, or deals with any other very difficult-to-sell subject matter, the likelihood is that you will not be much more successful in selling it than the overwhelming majority of those who have gone before you. The key thing to understand here is that the time you spend on writing a self-published book is all investment time.

It is not so easy to put a dollar-and-cents value on the time you spend writing a book, especially if you are a neophyte who has written the book on otherwise leisure time. An experienced author can make an over-simplified but useful estimate, though, which can be revealing to newer authors. Let us suppose that you have written a previous book of roughly the same kind as the one you now propose to write. That book ran 100,000 words—in manuscript 400 pages at a fairly standard 250 words per typed page. You were quite fast, both as writer and researcher, averaging about one page an hour of rough first-draft material and only fifteen minutes per page for all revisions. Overall, you averaged one hour and fifteen minutes per final manuscript page, for a total of 500 hours to produce your manuscript. That is about thirteen weeks of absolutely full-time, hard-driving work—or, more likely, a year of part-time work.

For illustrative purposes, let us assume that your publisher sold 5,000 copies of your hardcover book at $12.95 each and that your publishing contract provided for royalties of 10 percent of cover price for the first 5,000 copies sold. Your royalties were $1.295 per book times 5,000 books, for a total of $6,475. Your advance had been less than that, and your book had earned out—that is, its earnings at least equaled the advance royalties paid to you.

On the other hand, the book might have sold 10,000 copies, with royalties on the second 5,000 copies at 12½ percent of cover price, a usual arrangement for hardcover books. The additional royalty income would then be $8,094, for total royalty income of $14,569.

If the book had been a trade paperback rather than a hardcover, with typical royalty income of 6 percent of cover price on the first 10,000 copies and a probable price of $9.95 per book, then the royalty income on 5,000–10,000 copies would have been $2,985–$5,970.

Depending on sales, prices, and publishing form then, your range of income might have been anywhere from about $3,000 at the low end to about $15,000 on the high end. (For the occasional—and unpredictable—very successful book, the range would reach higher, of course.) In this instance, 500 hours of writing work might have been worth as little as $6 per hour and as much as $30 per hour. Assuming a median position, which is $18 per hour for 500 hours, then the foregone income for the self-publisher would, in this instance, be about $9,000. That is the roughest possible guess—but an instructive one. For if your self-published book does indeed "fall flat on its face," you are unlikely to get even your production costs back, much less any payment for your writing time, and the writing time will have been all dead loss in simple dollars-and-cents terms. Clearly, most authors, and certainly most self-publishing authors, do not write books for purely dollars-and-cents reasons—but it is important for authors to try to reach some sort of realistic time cost for writing.

Opportunity Costs

Looking at it a little differently, you might try to assess what income you might have generated by other means had you not written the book at all. What would those 500 hours have been worth had they been expended at other kinds of available remunerative work, as at your normal occupation? For some kinds of professionals, such as highly paid doctors and lawyers, 500 hours may be worth $50,000–$100,000. For someone otherwise unskilled, 500 hours may be worth as little as $2,000–$3,000. Seeing it that way, you are attempting to measure roughly what business analysts call *opportunity cost*.

This concept of opportunity cost also extends to the time you spend publishing your book. What you are doing when you self-publish is replacing all the time that is spent by a commercial publishers' employees with your own time; that may amount to hundreds of hours more, aside from the cash you spend to publish your book. Yes, it may be a labor of love and well worth every hour you spend, but you should try to place a dollars-and-cents figure on what those hours are worth in terms of possible other income foregone.

A third kind of opportunity cost is more easily measured. That is the foregone income on the cash you actually spend on the writing and publishing of your book, from money spent for the paper you put into your typewriter or word processor to the money you pay for professional help, composition, book manufacturing, mailing, promoting, and all the rest. You may easily spend $10,000 out of your own pocket to publish and market a modest quantity of your own books—and if you wish to do some serious promotion or produce a physically large hardcover book, you could spend a great deal more than that. Well, every dollar of your own you spend on publishing your book is a dollar that is not otherwise earning for you, over the period of, say, a year from the completion of manuscript to the first dollar you receive from sales of your book. When available interest rates on tax-free municipal bonds are in the 10 percent range, or stocks are yielding in an after-tax 10 percent range, then the opportunity cost or lost income on each dollar spent in publishing is ten cents. On $10,000 you invested in self-publishing, you may lose $1,000 in foregone income if your book does not earn back the cash you have put into it. Don't ever think that if you invest a dollar and get a dollar back a year later you have "broken even." It doesn't work that way. The dollar you get back at the end of that year—if you get it back—is worth less than the dollar you put in, by whatever the rate of inflation was that year and does not include the earnings you might have made from it.

But many author-publishers do not have all that much in the way of liquid assets. Like so many others who develop small business enterprises, they must borrow and pay interest on those borrowings. Sometimes, it does not seem like borrowing at all, as when they simply extend and roll over existing debts and use credit card and bank account overdraft privileges. But that is borrowing, too, just as much as when you borrow money from a bank or add to a mortgage on your house. And borrowing costs money—not the 9 to 12 percent you might expect to pay a lender if you were a major corporation borrowing at the "prime rate," but the 15 to 25 percent you can expect to pay as a small borrowers, your interest varying with economic conditions and the kind of borrowing used. During the year in which your self-publishing venture is all outgo and no income, you can reasonably expect every $10,000 you borrow to cost you $1,500–$2,500 in interest. That is a very real out-of-pocket cost, not an opportunity cost.

Start-up and Overhead Costs

Some other cash outlays are inescapable start-up costs, including initial legal and accounting fees, a minimal amount of stationery, and some basic reference books. For limitation of liability, tax avoidance, business credit, and other such reasons, you will be wise to organize your publishing enterprise as a corporation. You could do the necessary corporate organization and paper-filing yourself to save a little money, but we would recommend using a lawyer and having a qualified public accountant or certified public accountant help you set up your books. You should really not figure your start-up costs of this kind at much less than $500–$1,000.

Among the other continuing inescapable overhead costs, there are some corporate taxes to pay, whether or not you make money; some accounting or bookkeeping fees; and some additional tax returns. Later, if you hire any people, there will be Federal and state forms to file, withholding taxes, and more tax returns and accounting fees. For some self-publishers, it will also be wise to purchase libel insurance. You should not reasonably expect to spend much less than $1,000 a year for these kinds of ongoing overhead costs, no matter how small your incorporated self-publishing enterprise.

Editorial Costs

Many other kinds of costs are much more variable, depending upon such matters as the kind of book you write, how much and what kind of freelance assistance you hire, what mode of composition you choose, what manufacturing decisions are made, and how much marketing money you choose to spend.

The first of these kinds of widely varying costs relates to the hiring of editorial freelancers. A freelance professional developmental editor—who will work with you throughout the whole writing process, helping you shape and sharpen your work—may charge you by the hour, at rates ranging from $10–$20 an hour. Others may charge a flat fee per job, ranging anywhere from a few hundred dollars for a brief nonfiction work to as much as $3,000 or more to work with you very deeply on the editing and virtual rewriting of a substantial novel or nonfiction work.

A ghostwriter—someone who actually writes the book in large part while you supply the substance of the material in the work—will need a good deal of cash for the large amount of time expended, which is likely to be expressed in a flat fee rather than an hourly rate. If you do use a ghostwriter, by the way, it is probably best to do it on a flat-rate basis, for a ghostwriter is an author, and authors have a hard time predicting how much time a piece of work will take to write well no matter how experienced they are. An even modestly experienced writer will charge you at least $3,000–$5,000 for "ghosting" a small work and ghostwriting fees often range up to three or four times as much as that. "Star" ghostwriters will very often want their names on books as co-authors, a substantial share of royalties, and fees or advances against royalties of tens of thousands of dollars; most self-publishing authors are unlikely to even attempt to enter into arrangements with such high-priced ghostwriters.

Freelance copyeditors hired to lightly edit your work and prepare it for composition will charge $6–$15 an hour, depending upon their experience and the current demand for their services. You can reasonably expect that a 400-page manuscript, running about 250 typed words per page, composed mostly of print and with little in the way of figures, will take a good copyeditor 40–70 hours to do. Complex and difficult-to-read work will take longer, sometimes perhaps as much as half again as long to copyedit well. Remember that if you want to discuss and dispute copyediting changes, additional re-editing charges will be generated.

Another kind of freelancer you want to hire during the publishing process is a picture researcher. If your book requires illustrations from other sources, you may find and secure those illustrations yourself, or you may hire a professional to find and secure the illustrations for you. Picture research can be a very considerable undertaking even for experienced authors, and many publishers and authors alike hire professionals in this area. If you do, you will probably pay that researcher $18–$20 per hour. (In years past, picture researchers sometimes set their fees at so much—say $15—per illustration finally selected, but few do so now.) It is very difficult to state any kind of average number of illustrations you can expect to secure for each hour of a picture researcher's work, as so much depends on the kind of material you are seeking and how much you are willing to pay for it.

Then there are the costs of illustrations themselves, whoever secures them. A black-and-white illustration, such as a newspaper or magazine photograph which is still covered by copyright, may cost $50–$100 or even more for a single use in your book. A color photo in copyright may cost more than that. On the other hand, Dover Publications and several other publishers issue many books full of out-of-copyright illustrations; these are of high enough quality to be used as is, and may therefore cost less than a dollar each if you use several illustrations taken from the same book. Many other illustrations, especially those created by government sources, are not covered by copyright but are in the public domain; for these you may need to pay modest fees, perhaps $5–$15 per illustration, for copies suitable for reproduction. In addition, some museums charge anywhere from a few dollars to as much as $50–$75 per illustration for permission to use the illustration in your book; commercial illustration houses may charge even more. You may use no researched illustrations at all, or just a few that are free for the taking and easy to find. But if you want to do a heavily illustrated book carrying many in-copyright works, you will be wise to hire an experienced picture researcher. A professional researcher will not only find the desired illustrations more efficiently but is quite likely to save you a good deal of money besides, even after his or her fee. We will go into the whole process of picture research later in this book, but for now let us point out that an experienced researcher will often be able to find out-of-copyright and publicly owned illustrations that will suit your needs just as well as the very expensive in-copyright illustrations you are likely to see first.

Assume that you want fifty illustrations for your book, that none are impossibly difficult to secure, and that about ten indispensable ones are in copyright. If you use a picture researcher, you can reasonably expect to pay about $1,500 for the illustrations you want, give or take $500 or so. For some kinds of heavily illustrated books, you can also spend five to ten times that amount; or your book may require only a couple of hundred dollars all told for ten to twenty easily secured, but perhaps very beautiful, classic photos from public domain archives.

You may want original photos or illustrations for your book. If such material forms an important part of the work and you are not a professional photographer or illustrator, then the best thing you can do is team up with one to do the book. Then the book becomes a self-publishing partnership with both of you sharing risks and rewards.

If, on the other hand, you want to hire a photographer, you can reasonably expect to have to pay at least $50 per photo, plus expenses if travel is involved, for a photograph to be used in the body of the book; photographs to be used on a book cover will more generally cost you $300 or more, especially if they are in color. A talented illustrator can be expected to charge $15–$100 per illustration, or even more, depending on the complexity of the work.

Maps and complex line drawings may cost out-of-pocket money, too. You may be able to do maps yourself with the help of looseleaf maps in the public domain, which can be copied at the public library and used as base maps. If that will not do, then you can expect to pay an artist at least $50 for the simplest map, and $350–$500 for very complex maps involving much research and perhaps several colors.

You may hire a publishing services organization to contract out all of these editorial and illustration costs—as well as the rest of the costs right up to finished books and even beyond—or you may handle them all yourself. Either way, the functions and costs are there and must be understood and performed.

So, too, the design function. If you are doing a small, self-covered, saddlestitched pamphlet of your own poems, design may be little more than typing one short poem to a page and having a printer set type of your choice or just make plates for printing by photographing your typed papes or computer printouts. But if you are doing more—going from a 400-page manuscript to a softcover- or hardcover-bound book—then you need a book designer. That designer will work with all the elements—layout, type, paper, binding, cover, and all the rest—to design the complete package that will be the finished book. To do that kind of job, a professional in this area will charge you from as little as $750 for a very simple book to as much as $4,000.

You will also need design and art for a cover. That may be as simple and inexpensive as working with someone employed by your printer to cover or self-cover a small pamphlet—or as complex as working with artist and book designer to create a hardcover dust jacket or a paperback cover capable of competing for buyer attention in trade bookstores. For the latter, freelance help is likely to cost you about $300–$500 for the design itself, though a high-powered, fashionable designer would charge a good deal more. The actual preparation of the cover costs extra. These costs can be minimal, as when your cover design consists of type alone or of a public domain photograph; but if art is drawn or photographs are taken specially for the purpose, the cost could run into the thousands. Clearly this is not a recommended choice for self-publishers.

Composition Costs

Composition costs also vary widely, between kinds and sizes of books and the kinds of composition modes used. That same little book of poetry in typewriter type may cost nothing more than the time it takes you to type it—or it can cost a few pennies per poem for someone else to type it. The 400-page manuscript going into book form may be quite another matter, however. Let us first assume that you are going to do the conventional thing, which is to take the manuscript to a compositor, have it composed into columns of type, and then made up ready for printing into pages of type, with whatever illustrative material you wish inserted, all according to the book design you have specified.

Compositors normally charge by page of composed type, with per-page charges depending upon the amount of type they must put in the average page of the work, the complexity of the material in composition terms, and the difficulty of handling differently prepared kinds of copy. Your 400-page typed manuscript, without illustrations, may become 250 pages of anything from a 5½"x8" trade paperback to a large 7"x10" hardcovered book. If the setting is straightforward—without much in the way of numbers, diagrams, and charts, which printers call tabular matter—each page may cost in the $8–$18 range to compose, depending upon the compositor, the competitive situation in the area, your astuteness as a buyer and bid-securer, and whether or not you have hired a professional to handle the composition and manufacturing. Some very complex composition is far more costly, up into the $50–$100 per page range, with some tabular matter going even higher. Actually, unless you have special knowledge in these areas, we strongly urge you to have your book designer or publishing service organization handle this for you. That 250 pages of straight composition at $8–$18 per page comes to a composition cost of $2,000–$4,500.

Beyond that, there are corrections and page makeup. Those corrections that you can identify during proofreading as printer's errors (PEs) will cost you nothing to correct. Author's alterations (AAs) —those errors that are yours, and any additions and corrections you want to make at the galley stage—will be charged at the hourly rate previously agreed upon between you and the compositor for such work. Once in page proof, the cost of further changes will depend upon the kind of composition mode being used. If it is a computer composition, you may be able to make changes during the page proof stage at no more cost than before. If it is not, changes made once pages are made up and page proofs prepared can be prohibitively expensive.

Assuming you are using the conventional mode, after corrections in galley proofs, you will make up pages. That is an artist's work, whether that artist is your book designer, someone else secured by or working for your publishing services organization, or someone employed by your compositor. Often page makeup is included in the package of services you negotiate with your designer or compositor. If not, the additional cost for page makeup alone may run $2.50–$4.00 per page, especially with illustrations and art to be placed.

Computer Composition

An experimental new way to handle composition costs is to compose the book yourself, typing it onto a disc through your home computer and using that disc to drive composition equipment owned by a compositor, at hoped-for considerable savings. That mode may indeed emerge strongly in coming years as the many kinds of home computers and composing machines become increasingly compatible and as home computers equipped with printers and large capacity become integral multi-purpose installations in most American homes. In these years, however, there are two major drawbacks to this composition arrangement.

First, there is the problem of incompatibility. If you do have a home computer with all the requisite features, you still may have some difficulty in finding a printer who can work directly from your disc. As many prematurely hopeful authors working with large publishers have found in recent years, possession of a disc containing a book may be no better than possession of a typed manuscript. Authors wishing to present discs to publishers have all too often been asked to present a printout instead, so that publishers can submit manuscripts to incompatible printing systems for recomposition.

That problem will probably be solved within the next decade, perhaps even sooner. But for author-publishers, the problem of cost may not be solved so soon. For even with compatibility, it would be necessary to do a good deal of composition—far more than you would do on any one book—before it would be economical to purchase a home computer as a composing device. Once you figure in the cost of the necessary computer-printer setup, including direct costs as well as opportunity and interest costs, and when you have added some cost factor for your own unpaid labor, there is no way in the world that you can cost-justify home composition of a single self-published book. On the other hand a "computer buff" who already owns a good deal of expensive equipment acquired for other purposes may be able to add modestly or not at all to present equipment; find a printer with compatible equipment; justify the extra labor of composition as recreation and research; and be quite satisfied to home-compose a self-published book. And if such an author does several self-published books, increased savings may be available as the years go by. As of this writing, home computer composition seems to be a little early, in cost-effectiveness terms, except for people who are computer buffs.

Additional Costs

In between composition and manufacturing is another small cost wrinkle, having to do with bound galleys. If you want pre-publication reviews in the few review media aimed mainly toward the book trade, you will have to provide pre-publication books to review. This is normally done by providing uncorrected bound copies of the galleys of your book, without illustrations or index, so that reviews can be written and appear in time for booksellers to enter pre-publication orders. Bound galleys cost about $20–$30 each, and you will need five to ten of them if you decide to take this route. You may include the costs of proofs and galleys in the package of services you negotiate with the compositor; in any case, be sure to establish beforehand the number of sets of proofs you will be getting and what price you will have to pay for any additional sets, if desired.

Proofreading and indexing can also be additional costs at this stage if you choose not to perform those functions yourself. Professional proofreaders will generally charge $9–$12 per hour; indexers' rates are the same or slightly higher. Many indexers will, however, work on a flat fee if you have set specifications on the length and detail of the index you want. In any case, you should plan $500 or more in out-of-pocket costs for these two functions.

You may, of course, employ a complete service organization to handle all these functions for you, as well as to oversee the actual manufacturing of the book. Such professionals are likely to be able to obtain a better price for many functions, since they have established relationships with many freelancers and suppliers. Balanced against this are the additional costs for their own time and your possible desire to perform some or many of these functions yourself.

Manufacturing Costs

Then there are manufacturing costs, which are very directly a function of the book you want to produce. All the manufacturing choices you make are also cost choices. One kind of book may cost fifty cents per completely finished unit to manufacture; another may cost $50. It may cost only a dollar a book to turn your composed 400-page manuscript into some thousands of smallish trade paperbacks. It may cost $5 a book to turn the same composed 400-page manuscript into a rather large, quite substantial hardcover book.

Aside from income foregone while writing your book, manufacturing cost is the largest single kind of expenditure you are likely to make as a self-publisher. It is certainly your largest cash expenditure unless you involve yourself in heavy advertising and other promotional outlays. It is highly variable, though, and amounts spent will depend greatly on your other choices. If you spend one dollar a book to manufacture 500 very small paperbacks, you will be spending $500 on the first printing. If you spend five dollars per book to manufacture 5,000 rather expensive hardcover books, you will be spending $25,000 on first-run manufacturing costs. Those are very wide bounds and will become meaningful only when the choices to be made are better understood.

Cost per book tends to go down as manufacturing costs go up, primarily because there is less handling time per book on press as print runs get longer. But total cash costs go up as more books are produced. Five thousand copies of a rather standard-sized hardcover book made out of your 400-page manuscript, and without very many illustrations, may cost you $1.50–$2.00 per book to manufacture, on top of all other costs. That is $7,500–$10,000. On the other hand, 1,000 copies of the same book, which is about as few as you would print if you seriously planned to try to sell the book in even the smallest set of markets, might cost almost twice as much per book, but less than half as much in total dollars. One thousand books at $2.75–$3.75 is $2,750–$3,750 for manufacturing. Bear in mind that the numbers themselves will vary greatly in each specific situation and that paperback numbers work a little differently than hardcover numbers. But the relationships between these sets of manufacturing costs remain basically the same.

Marketing Costs

On the marketing side, there are fewer irreducible out-of-pocket expenditures than on the writing, editing, and manufacturing sides. However, you are likely to spend a good deal of valuable time taking your book to market, no matter how inexpensively you do so. You may need time to create advertising and publicity; to show and tell potential buyers about your book at meetings, exhibits, readings, and lectures; to sell your book to booksellers and wholesalers; and to create brochures and direct-mail selling packages if you market in that way. All require varying levels of expenditure—but all take considerable amounts of your own time, no matter how much professional help you get along the way. Do not be surprised if you find yourself spending hundreds of hours selling your book after you have written it and taken it all the way through the publication process to finished book. That is a cost, to be evaluated in dollars and cents, just as you evaluated the cost of writing your book. And this is a cost that for many authors is not offset by the psychic rewards that come from writing and producing a book. Some authors do enjoy the recognition that can come with having a book out, but one of the main hazards connected with publishing and selling your own book is the possibility that you may find yourself working hard at the relatively uncongenial pursuit of marketing, rather than moving swiftly to start writing another book.

Some irreducibly minimal marketing costs are involved in any serious attempt to sell your book. These would include small printing costs for such materials as publicity releases and a printed piece describing your book for booksellers and wholesalers. Telephone costs will very quickly mount to a couple of hundred dollars, as you make necessary long-distance calls. There are extra automobile expenses as you move about in your extended local area selling your book to booksellers and others. Marketing and business correspondence will entail other costs—postage, large envelopes, and probably some typing and other clerical help. For all these kinds of functions you should expect to spend at least $500–$1,000 if you are going to try to sell your book at all effectively. Hiring a professional publicist costs more—how much more depends on what you want that publicist to do for and with you.

Advertising and direct-mail selling are also mainly variables, for in those areas what you spend on both freelance help and on the process itself relates directly to the kind of book you are doing and to available budgets and anticipated results. Bear in mind that any meaningful advertising and mail selling, even to narrow or regional markets, is bound to be expensive as related to the total publishing budget for a self-published book. The key word here is *meaningful*. To produce and place inadequate, amateurish advertising is to throw away whatever money you spend. To produce and send poorly done direct-mail pieces to the wrong prospective purchasers or to too few prospective purchasers is to waste your mailing money.

Handling Costs

Additional costs are connected with the straightforward business-handling side of the self-publishing business, costs connected with shipping, billing, collecting, and recordkeeping. People new to the book business are often surprised at just how costly it is to ship books to booksellers and individual bookbuyers. For example, your 400-page manuscript, now turned into a 250-page standard-sized book, will be likely to weigh one to one-and-a-half pounds in hardcover, or one-half to three-quarters pounds in trade paperback.

As of this writing, it will cost you about a dollar to surface mail a single copy of that hardcover book anywhere in the United States, which includes postage and the cost of mailing materials but does not include any allowance for the labor involved, whether yours or cash out of pocket you pay someone else. The paperback will cost about 75¢ to mail on the same basis. If you use United Parcel Service—which is faster and surer, but more expensive—the hardcover book will cost $1.50–$2.10 to surface ship, depending upon where you send it in the United States, and the paperback will cost 20¢–40¢ less.

Multiple book shipments cost considerably less per book. Assuming that your hardcover book weighs one-and-a-half pounds, twenty copies will weigh thirty pounds. At 63¢ for the first pound, 23¢ for pounds 2–7, and 14¢ per pound thereafter, up to a maximum of seventy pounds per package—the rates as of this writing—thirty pounds of books will cost you $5.23 to mail. If you add the cost of shipping materials, you would get perhaps $6 in all, or about 40¢ for each of the fifteen books mailed. UPS charges for the same shipment would probably average about the same, as UPS charges go up with weight much more slowly than postal charges, making UPS by far the better way to go for larger quantities of books because of its relative speed and reliability.

Storage of books may or may not be an out-of-pocket cost. Many author-publishers store their book stock in their own homes. For those who hire storage space, the cost of storage for at least a year should be figured into costs. With the increase in self-publishing, more and more printers and binderies are also offering fulfillment services for both storage and handling. That is a route you may want to explore, although the additional costs and delays in handling may militate against using such services.

On the financial side, there is the cost of billing and often re-billing—as well as telephone collection efforts when rebillings have proven fruitless. If you ultimately hire a collection agency, there is the foregone income from the agency's cut of whatever collection is made. Finally, there is the lost income from a totally uncollectible account—and there are always some, in any business.

Some hidden costs are connected with credit and collection. When others buy from you and you must await payment for several months—as so often occurs when booksellers are slow in paying small publishers—then the cost of either opportunity cost or interest must be figured into your costs. Someone who owes you $1,000 is costing you, for example, ¾ of 1 percent per month, or $9 per $1,000 per month—if 9 percent is what you might otherwise earn relatively safely on your money. If that owing goes on for six months, your opportunity cost is $54 per $1,000. If, on the other hand, you are borrowing that $1,000 to finance your self-publishing business, then your very real cash-out-of-pocket interest cost is likely to be 1.5 percent per month, or $18 per $1,000 per month; that comes to a very real $108 in interest you have had to pay in six months.

Looking at it a little differently, let us assume that you are floating your self-publishing business on borrowed money, on which you are paying 18 percent annual interest. You are selling a book which retails at $15 to retailers and jobbers for an average price of $8. For every $8 owed you for six months, you are therefore paying 9 percent, or 75¢, in interest. That is a great deal, relative to the economics of self-publishing a single book, and a figure to be taken into account very carefully.

Most of these costs, such as shipping, have nowhere to go but up. The figures given in this chapter, as throughout this book, are very general ranges, supplied only so that you will have some real-

istic insight into the kinds of costs self-publishers encounter and
the relative sizes of these costs, one to the other. For that purpose,
they have been summarized in Table 2, which shows a range of
costs that might be involved in self-publishing 5,000 copies of a
trade paperback, composed mostly of text, from a manuscript running 400 pages and averaging 250 words per page. In some parts
of the country, with luck and some very careful shopping and
bargaining, you might arrange to pay less for some of these services.
Elsewhere, if you make elaborate, expensive choices, you could pay
even more. The point here is to realize that the self-publishing
decision—and all of the smaller decisions involved in the publishing process—can involve considerable costs and should not be one
taken lightly or unknowingly.

Table 2:
Range of costs for self-publishing 5,000 copies of a mostly text
manuscript (400 pages, at 250 words per page):

Author's writing time	$ 3,000–$15,000
Opportunity cost	1,500– 2,000
Start-up costs	500– 1,000
Overhead costs	0– 1,000
Developmental editor	250– 3,000
Copyeditor	240– 1,050
Illustrations	1,000– 2,000
Designer	750– 4,000
Cover design and art	300– 500
Composition	2,000– 4,500
Proofreading and indexing	0– 500
Manufacturing	7,500– 10,000
Marketing and office costs	500– 1,000
Shipping	2,000– 10,500
TOTAL	$11,250–$56,050

All these figures must be taken into account in fixing the final
price for your book. Though pricing is actually done during the
manufacturing stage of the publishing process, it is appropriate
to discuss it here, with the whole range of costs freshly in mind.

Pricing

For the self-publishing author, pricing is far more likely to be a matter of roughly approximating the prices of similar books in the marketplace than of soberly and precisely estimating costs, discounts, needed profit margins, and consequent selling prices. The plain truth is that, once you have realistically figured in all the kinds of costs we have previously discussed, including the relatively huge cost of all your time, and have made a reasonably conservative estimate of the number of books you are likely to sell, there is hardly any way in the world to anticipate profits out of self-publishing. You may hit a bonanza book, of course; but no one should self-publish with the aim of striking it rich with a single self-published book. That way lies great disappointment—and perhaps personal bankruptcy as well. Authors publishing through commercial houses should have no illusions either; very few books come even close to adequately compensating their authors for the amount of time put into the creation of the work. All of this has never stopped authors from authoring, however, or from finding ways to put their work into print, as self-publishers or through publication by others.

Most self-publishing authors are quite content to be able to take their books through the publication process into print and then out into the marketplace with a fair chance of getting their out-of-pocket cash expenditures back and something more for their time. The pricing of self-published books should properly aim at those quite achievable goals, not the profit goals that must be sought by commercial publishers. That can be a considerable advantage in the marketplace; for example, self-publishers of narrow-market professional, academic, and reference works need not price themselves out of some of their natural markets, as some well-established commercial professional and reference publishers are very notably and shortsightedly doing in this period.

But that does not mean pricing your book much lower than those around it in a bookstore or much lower than similar books offered by mail or sold off the lecture platform. People buy books for many reasons, only one of which is price; and a too-low price may not even help sales of your book. The main thing is to charge a competitive price for your book, rather than one so high that it may make people hesitate at the moment of making what may be an impulsive buying decision.

Take, for example, that smallish, softcover book of poetry we have discussed. It may have cost very little to set in type, print, and bind, and you may have used no freelance assistance at all, except that one of your friends supplied several lovely drawings in return for a small share of the proceeds, if any. It may be set in typewriter type; or more likely on a home computer equipped with an appropriate word-processing program. It is quite possible that you have put no more than perhaps $1,000 in cash into it, including composition, print, bindery, and even the small amounts you have spent on a homemade press release, some extra gasoline and telephone expenses, and perhaps even a few small ads in a regional poetry magazine, a college or alumni publication, and a very local newspaper. For that $1,000, you may have 1,000 copies of a modest trade paperback in hand, some hundreds of which have been placed in local book outlets and the rest of which you plan to sell at poetry readings and perhaps through a small mailing to friends and other poets. You plan to make any further cash promotional expenditures entirely out of whatever cash beyond your $1,000 cash investment you earn from sales.

One very normal tendency in that situation is to price the book at something like $2.95, even after 40 percent bookstore discounts, which will yield you nearly twice what each of those 1,000 books has actually cost you in out of pocket cash. And those you sell yourself at full price will yield almost triple your cash cost, even though those you sell by mail will not yield quite as much because of the cost of mailing.

That is entirely sound thinking, given your very low cash costs—but it may be too low a price to charge. A trip to the local bookstore may show you similar books selling at $3.95–$7.95, and sometimes even more, which means that the market will bear a higher price than you thought to charge. And you may need the higher price, for you may print 1,000 books but sell only a few hundred. Think of it this way: if you price your book at $2.95 and sell half through booksellers at 40 percent off and half at poetry readings at full price, your average revenue per book is $2.36, and you have to sell 424 to get your $1,000 in cash out of pocket back. But if you price it at $5.95 and that price is competitive in the marketplace, you need sell only 210. You may not be able to sell 424 books of poetry, but you should be able to get your money back out of at least 210 sales just to people who know and admire you and your work.

This is, of course, all very elementary, but it is important to see it clearly, for far too many writers habitually allow themselves to be put off by the "mysteries" of the publishing business; those mysteries are really only very basic small business matters and numbers, somewhat less complicated than those encountered every day by the people running the local small grocery store. In the instance above, the only real business mistakes the poet can make are to price too low and to print too many. Proper pricing and competent marketing by reaching for natural personal, local, and special-interest markets will get the poet's cash back, and probably then some.

The numbers and necessities work in basically the same fashion for somewhat more complex and expensive self-published books as well.

Within certain bounds, however, marketing considerations have more to do with pricing than do costs. Like commercial publishers, self-publishing authors will, to a large extent, price their general books or special-interest works to suit the marketplace. A general-interest trade paperback, for example, might be priced at $12.95 if that is the usual price for other comparable books. On the other hand, a book that is physically the same but aimed at a well-defined special-interest market, especially a professional book or an academic work, may be priced at twice that.

Size of Printing

Closely intertwined with the questions of cost, pricing, and marketing is the size of printing appropriate to the self-published book. Earlier we talked of a self-publishing author who sold 5,000 copies of a $12.95 trade paperback, mostly through direct platform-selling efforts, after having spent a total of $21,660 to produce those 5,000 copies. That author did extremely well, as the average sales of those books was at 90 percent of cover price and selling costs were small.

Now take the same basic example but make the book a somewhat more general book, with the same price and 5,000 sales, but with 2,000 sold in bookstores, 1,000 by direct mail, and 2,000 to libraries. Assume somewhat higher promotional costs, because the book is a more general book. Assume also that those 1,000 mail sales at full price have cost something to make, even though they were to small, particularly responsive lists. (You will not be selling a single $12.95 book to mass lists, as the economics just won't work for you.) Shipping and associated business costs will also be larger. Say total cash expenditures are $25,000. Your 2,000 bookstore sales will yield you an average of 45 percent of cover price, for now you are also selling to chains and jobbers, who get more than the individual bookseller's 40 percent discount, and partly through distributors, who also get their share. (For the purpose of this rough costing-pricing example, we will assume no returns, figuring that you will sell any returns later on, rather than having to remainder or destroy them.) Your revenue from the 2,000 bookstore sales is therefore $11,655.

Your 2,000 library sales are at an average of 80 percent of full price, as you are selling mostly through library distributors, and your revenue from those sales is therefore $20,720. Your 1,000 mail sales yield $12,950, which, when added together with the other figures, adds up to total revenue of $45,325, close to twice what your out-of-pocket expenses were. With that mix of sales, your average revenue per book is $9.07. So to break even on cash out-of-pocket, you needed to sell not 5,000 books, but only 2,756 to get your cash back.

Total cash expenditure	$25,000
Revenue on 5,000 copies sold	
Bookstores: 2,000 x $12.95 per	
copy x 45 percent (discount)	$11,655
Libraries: 2,000 x $12.95 per	
copy x 80 percent (discount)	20,720
Mail sales: 1,000 x $12.95 per copy	12,950
Total revenue	$45,325

Average revenue per book = $45,325 ÷ 5,000 copies = $9.07
Breakeven = $25,000 ÷ $9.07 = 2,756 copies sold

But "only" 2,756 books can be a lot of books if nobody is buying. And $25,000 invested in cash out-of-pocket, on top of all the time you have put in, can be an enormous amount. With that in mind, you will want to print 2,000–3,000 books at the start, rather than 5,000; you will also be wise to budget promotional expenditures very carefully, doing some of your spending only out of cash generated from book sales. You can probably bring the same book to market, having used the same kind of professional help, for something like $15,000, spending the rest as needed. Then, using the same assumptions, you would need sell only 1,654 books to get your cash out.

If total cash expenditures were $15,000, and the average revenue per book was $9.07, breakeven would be $15,000 ÷ $9.07 = 1,654 copies sold

---

The one thing you will not want to do, unless competitive prices force you to do so, is charge much less. It is unlikely to make you able to sell very many more books and can make it far harder to get your money out. And, if you have guessed wrong about the "mix" of your sales between bookstores, libraries, direct mail, and personal direct sales, you may need far more sales than you realized. That bookstore sale can be relied upon to give you only about 45 percent of cover price, and often much less if you have to take back and ultimately remainder or destroy returns. If the foregoing example were to assume only bookstore and library sales, 90 percent to bookstores and 10 percent to libraries (not at all an unrealistic set of assumptions for many books), then your average revenue per sale would be $6.28, and you would need 2,389 sales just to get your cash out. It would be a little more than that, really, as shipping and associated costs would be larger; these figures are rough approximations, and only that.

If yours were a narrow-market book, you could very probably charge more, sell at a much higher average price, and find yourself getting your cash out at a much lower number of sales. The author putting $12,000 in cash into the creation of 2,000 professional books which can successfully be priced at $24.95, and will

Total cash expenditures = $15,000
Total sales: 5,000 copies
  Bookstores: 4,500 x $12.95 x 45 percent = $26,224
  Libraries: 500 x $12.95 x 80 percent =   5,180

Total revenue $31,404
Average revenue per book = $31,404 ÷ 5,000 = $6.28
Breakeven = $15,000 ÷ $6.28 = 2,389 copies

yield $22.00 in publishing revenue each, need only sell 545 books to get his or her cash out.

In each instance, the publishing choice, cost, and price elements work together to form the publishing situation: the publishing choice is central, followed by astute costing and pricing decisions, always much enhanced by securing sound professional advice. If, after examining all these elements, you feel that your book stands a reasonable chance of earning back the money you put into it, plus giving you personal satisfaction, you may well decide to try your hand at self-publishing your first or next book. For that, we will start at the very beginning of the publishing process, with the conception and development of the book.

CHAPTER 4

☆

From Idea to Finished Manuscript

If you want a good book, rather than merely a published book, you have to be able to do for yourself—or get one or more freelance professionals to do for you—what a publisher will do for you on the editorial side.

Let us be very clear that you can, if you work hard enough at it, certainly learn how to do it all yourself. Anaïs Nin, among others, learned how to do every aspect of publishing, from conception right through to running the printing press—and produced very creditable short runs of books that are now collector's items. Many artistically successful—and even a few commercially successful—small presses have been built just that way, by people with very little money and a craving to publish.

But let us also be very clear that most authors bent on publishing their own work will profit greatly by judicious help from competent professionals at every step of the publishing way. If you are not bent on doing it all on your own, and can afford it, by all means include such help in your self-publishing effort; you'll probably get a considerably better book out of it.

In any case, as an author-publisher, you will need to be thoroughly familiar with all phases of publishing, even if you do not perform all the functions yourself. In this chapter, we will outline the main steps in the editorial process, from the conception of the book to a completed, fully edited and copyedited manuscript ready for composition—or, if you are composing as you write and edit on a word processor, from conception to composed material ready for makeup into pages prior to printing. They do not always occur in the order discussed here, nor is the process often as tidy as the sequence here provided. A great deal of back and forth occurs between author and editor, and the timing and sequence of editorial events depends greatly on the kind of book being done, the experience of the author, and matters of personal style and the chemistry between editor and author. But whether you try to do it all yourself or get some professional editorial assistance, these editorial steps are necessary if you want to do a book that is as good as anything that might be done by a professional publisher. And you should want to do nothing less, within whatever constraints are imposed by available time and money. Indeed, it is quite possible that with such help your self-published book will be far better than if it had been done by most commercial publishers today; many of them in pursuit of profit cut corners and give authors far less editorial support than they did as recently as a decade ago, and far less than author-publishers are able to secure for themselves.

The Conception

Experienced authors, editors and publishers know that there is a long distance between book idea and publishable book idea. In some ways, it is as long as the distance between fully conceived idea and the finished manuscript itself. For the truth is that any group of experienced people can come up with a couple of dozen seemingly perfectly good book ideas in any longish meeting, as can any experienced author alone. On reflection, some of these books will turn out to have been done by others (though that does not always foreclose the idea); others may be intrinsically so difficult to do that their writing and other costs are prohibitive. But even the ideas not so hindered always need a good deal of thought and development before they are whipped into publishable form. That is why experienced editors want as much as they can get from authors proposing books for publication, including a full written outline of the book, a description of its probable audiences, a tentative annotated table of contents, and some sample material. Some editors demand far too much sample material—up to several chapters of a proposed book—and experienced authors resist those excessive sample material demands as wasteful of irreplaceable writing time.

But no experienced author or editor doubts the need to spend a good deal of time at hard, effective thinking about and shaping of a book idea before moving to create the book itself. That is so whether you publish your own book or place it with a commercial publisher. Occasionally, a reasonably good book is conceived quickly and written in a fine romantic frenzy; but that is a rare occurrence. Far more often, the book that is insufficiently considered and poorly planned turns out far too short, far too long, misshapen, or impossible to carry forward at some rather early stage. There may or may not be such a thing as "writer's block"; there is surely the writer's paralysis that almost inevitably develops from working on a badly conceived piece of work, and is treated as some kind of mysterious ailment.

Some short pieces may be a little different. A short poem, a short story, a brief essay—these may seem to spring full blown and ready to put on paper whole. They seldom do, really. Most likely the process of thinking them through happens obscurely, unconsciously or semi-consciously, and you are not aware of having planned the work that appears so marvelously before you. But setting out to write a book is quite a different matter.

The best way to go about it is to behave as if you really were planning to submit a book proposal to an editor at a publishing house. Not necessarily a large commercial publisher, where there would be an overriding need to submit a work thought to be commercially viable; you might be submitting a proposal to a professional and reference publisher, which can make money on a very short run of a certain kind of book, to a small press that has fewer strictures about profit margins, or to a university press that will publish books that are not necessarily for profit.

You may, indeed, want to submit such a book proposal to one or more publishers, if only to attempt to get a professional reaction to your fully conceived book idea. If you are inexperienced in publishing, you may want to hire an experienced editor to evaluate your proposal, whether you want to publish through others or on your own. Your self-publishing decision should still be entirely your own, but tempered by consideration of professional reactions to your proposal. You would certainly by terribly unwise to conceive a book idea, and proceed directly to the writing of the book.

Outlines and Samples

The first substantial step is to describe what the book will be about in as little as a paragraph and in not more than a single page. The book will change a good deal as you later write it, but the first clear-headed full description is indispensable. Without it, you cannot see or reach your audience, and that will usually make your book's contents far more diffuse than you would like—making it also very difficult to sell your book. If you find that you cannot clearly describe the book, then you probably have not thought the matter through well enough to properly start the book. Sometimes, writing a few sample passages will help focus your thinking, as will working at it from several different points of view. You should not actually start writing the book, however, until it has come sufficiently into focus for you to be able to fully describe it to yourself and others. A novelist may work with situations, fictional biographies and autobiographies, and descriptive material of all kinds, and may write shorter pieces that help the projected longer work come into focus, much as a painter may work with several kinds of studies before moving into the creation of a major painting. A historian may outline, write shorter essays, and develop different sets of propositions and models before starting a major work, as may several other kinds of nonfiction writers. A cookbook writer or encyclopedist may write several short pieces, for style, length, and form of entry before the projected work can properly come into focus.

In conceiving and focusing a book it is also important to allow enough time to let an idea simmer and "season." An idea may be a perfectly good one, though perhaps in need of some adjusting, but be abandoned too soon. It cannot be said too strongly that in this area nothing is wasted. As with all writing, save every scrap of paper you work on, and file it well enough to be able to locate it when you want it—you will very often find some use for it. Book ideas do not die, no matter how often they are put aside. They season; they transmute; they ultimately emerge anew, though perhaps changed so much that you can perceive little more than the germ of the initial idea.

Description in hand, you should pause to consider whether or not the book is feasible, where that question is appropriate. For a book of your poems, or for most novels, the question of feasibility scarcely arises; if you want to do the book enough, you will do it. But some scientific and technical books may not be feasible for those without sufficient mathematical and scientific background, just as a book on the whole history of humanity may be quite beyond someone without sufficient basic background.

Feasibility can be a matter of practical size, as well. Sometimes, the book you want to write may be beyond time and means, as in the instance of that history of humanity. Some books are very hard to do meaningfully in a compass brief enough to make them practical. Even a major multi-generational family saga, which might be entirely practical for someone else, may not be feasible for you, given your writing speed, level of experience, and available time.

Feasibility may also be, to a considerable extent, a matter of marketplace realities. If 200 books on the same aspect of computer language that you mean to cover have appeared in the last three years, your book may not be at all feasible in the marketplace, for you or anyone else, no matter how well you write your book or how original you mean to make it.

But feasibility is not a cut-and-dried matter. A book may at first seem too difficult, too large, or too much like many other books, but often can be modified early in its conception, becoming feasible while remaining a book you very much want to do. The scientific and technical work may become a popular book that lucidly explains otherwise obscure matters to a lay audience—and may be the book you wanted to do all along. The history of humanity may become a much better-focused work on an aspect of history that may appeal to you enormously, as a result no longer posing size or research problems. The redundant computer book may become unique and appealing with the addition of some kind of twist that appeals to a particular audience.

In this very early conceiving period, you should carefully consider your audience, unless your book is intended only for yourself and a few who are close to you. If you are consciously going to do a book that will sell only to very narrow markets, that decision may deeply affect your writing choices, as well as many other economic and esthetic choices. For example, an academic may do a rather substantial, heavily researched, densely written book for an audience of other academics and libraries, and be intellectually, esthetically, and economically satisfied by the resulting work and its performance in the marketplace. The same work, not so sharply focused and more popularly written, may satisfy neither professional nor lay audiences—nor its writer, being too narrow for general audiences, while being too imprecise and superficial for professional readers. Falling between two stools, the book may also not do well in the marketplace.

Similarly, but from the other end of the spectrum, a book aimed directly at popular audiences can be fatally stricken by cumbersome academic writing and the dense apparatus of scholarship. For popular work, it is best to leave the jargon at home altogether, and put the footnotes at the back of the book, where they will not get in the way of the narrative flow of the text. At the start, then, consider your audience.

Intentions, feasibility, and audience in mind, you should write a good brief description of your audience—those you think likely to buy the book—as you would for a publisher considering your book proposal. Since you are both author and publisher, you must consider carefully how you will sell your book and to whom. This may affect your writing—and your whole decision to self-publish or not. We will discuss marketing later in this book, but as an author-publisher, you will need to have marketing considerations firmly in mind throughout the publishing process.

Then it becomes desirable to expand your basic description of the work to an outline of your proposed book. For a work of fiction, that will be a descriptive outline. For a work of nonfiction, the descriptive outline may be best organized in the form of a tentative table of contents.

The one-page description captures your whole book idea. The descriptive outline casts and thereby captures the book itself. Although it and the book are likely to change greatly as you write, it is unwise to take your working outline too lightly. Develop a satisfying working outline, one you are fairly confident of working and living with as the book develops; the odds are that your work is conceptually flawed if you cannot do that before serious writing starts. On the other hand, it is possible to come close, but not quite to your satisfaction, and then move on to write some sample material if you have not already done so. Sometimes, what has been opaque in the conception becomes clear in the writing of sample material. Many writers move back and forth between early brief book description, descriptive outline, and sample material, repeatedly amending each element as the book is shaped. When you take your book proposal to a publisher, you have really shaped your book, subject to later changes as you write it. You should do no less for yourself, if you are to be a successful author-publisher.

Feasibility, in its several aspects, is raised once again in the outline. What may have seemed like a wonderful idea described on a single sheet of paper may, in extended outline, seem inadequately conceived. For example, many writers going from brief description to full outline find they have less to say than they had supposed; sometimes a seemingly good book idea turns into a magazine article or short story. The outline enables you to organize, structure, and proportion the several elements of the projected book; then you can see more clearly the probable size and shape of your book—and whether you really have a book there at all.

The sample material you write has at least as much to contribute to the development of the proposed work as the extended outline. In the sample, you are able to address the internal structuring of one or more substantial pieces of your work. The sample does much more than that, though. It tells you—and whoever you may be working with—a great deal about your writing and about the kind of writing you will need for the work in hand. No matter how good your planning, your writing work will fail if you have no ear for the language appropriate for the book and its audience. This is not a matter of grammar and spelling, by the way, although abysmally poor grammar and spelling usually indicate lack of ear or feel for the language. Copyediting can easily repair minor grammar and spelling errors, and professional writers generally avoid getting bogged down on those kinds of problems during the early stages of writing. But writing that is diffuse, unfocused, hopelessly pedantic, cliche-ridden, or so high-blown as to become laughable may be work that is beyond fixing by a copyeditor. And—at as basic a level as there is in writing—the aspiring author who cannot form a sensible sentence or string several sentences together so that they make a coherent paragraph needs more help than any editor can provide. The idea may still be feasible, but the book may then have to come from its creator through the head and hands of a skilled ghostwriter or acknowledged co-author. And if that is the case, you want to know it as early in the game as possible, to avoid a great deal of wasted time and frustration.

Your sample material can be drawn from anywhere in the proposed book. Most inexperienced authors naturally look to Chapter One for sample material, reasoning that the right way to do it is to start at the beginning. Not so. The first chapter of a book normally states the thesis and all the main elements of the book and is therefore often by far the most difficult chapter of the book to capture in the early stages. Much becomes clear in the writing, and the very tentative first chapter you prepare as a guide to writing may change a dozen times before you are finished with the book and be really completed only after the first draft of the rest of the book has been done. It is therefore usually best to take your sample material from later on in the book. Choose a specific section that stands rather independently, so that your writing can focus on such matters as tone, language, and internal structuring. This applies to nonfiction, rather than most fiction. Most fiction will depend so much on the early building of character and situation that Chapter One is the logical choice for selection of sample material.

You should write as much sample material as you and anyone you are working with need to properly evaluate the idea you are turning into a book. For rather experienced people that may sometimes be as little as a few pages, which (along with a basic description and an extended table of contents) serves to tell all that needs to be known before starting the book itself. Many professional writers quite properly regard this early casting of the book as the most important period of all, feeling that they have the book halfway written once they have it understood and fully cast; they work and rework contents and sample material again and again, and at considerable length, before they are satisfied and ready to start the book itself. Inexperienced authors should almost always cast the book this way, for this hard, long, and often seemingly unproductive early work can make much of the difference between a rather good book and a very bad one—or between a good book and no book at all. For a badly conceived and prepared book can—and all too often does—take years of hard and increasingly anguished work until it is ultimately abandoned by its devastated author.

Gauging Book Length

In doing the outline and sample, it is valuable to pay close attention to the relative importance—and therefore the probable sizes—of the book's main elements. The outline makes it possible to see internal structure and the relationships of the parts of each other and to the whole book. The sample makes it possible to begin to see how you want to say your piece and how many words you will need to say it.

Using a standard office typewriter—one that has pica type—and a fairly standard 60-character-wide line, you should produce a manuscript that will average 250 words per page. Typing all the way to the edge of the page, and down the page to the last possible line, you may cram in an average of 300 or even 325 words per page, but that leaves you no space for editorial comments and revisions. When producing a manuscript for yourself or others, your average should be more like the 250-word page.

A standard-sized hardcover or trade paperback book set in reasonably readable type will carry as little as 300 and as many as 450 words on its average page.

The probable size of your book deserves close attention, for—from the author-publisher's point of view—words are costs. Words are time; they are also composition, paper, bindery, shipping, and mailing costs. The bigger the book, the bigger these costs. Yes, you can cut the size of a book by using smaller type; but a good book in small, hard-to-read type may hardly be worth publishing, which places built-in limitations on the savings that can be achieved in that way.

Therefore, a manuscript of about 200 pages will result in a 50,000-word book, which is about the low end of the book-size range. A 50,000–125,000-word book, which is the main range for most full-sized standard works, will be about 200–500 typed pages in manuscript.

From these figures and your outline and sample, you can make a rough word-count projection for your book. Assuming that you have projected a ten-chapter book, and your sample chapter—which you consider average—turns out to be forty typed pages long, you are likely to have a book of 400 manuscript pages or 100,000 words, well within the average range.

But if, as so often happens, your chapter turns out to be ten pages long, then you are projecting a manuscript of 100 pages, or 25,000 words, which is far too short. There may not be a full-sized book there at all—or you may not have developed the work as fully as you should have. Many writers write too tight, without enough detail and illustrative prose. Put more roundly and fully, the work may indeed be a full-sized book, and a good one.

On the other hand, your sample chapter may turn out to be 100 pages long, which would project into a mammoth 1,000-page, 250,000-word manuscript. That may be far too much book—for your audience, for your time, and for your pocketbook. Even very experienced authors can run into great difficulty on matters of length of book. In one classic instance, a seasoned reference book staff produced an encyclopedia far greater than its projected size between A and F, and then found itself forced to cram the rest of the alphabet into just a few remaining volumes. Yet some modest conceptual changes and astute editing may result in a manageable book. The main need is to create a careful outline and sample material early enough to gauge the size and proportion of the whole, avoiding these kinds of pitfalls.

At this stage, you may also want to do some quite preliminary thinking on the possible inclusion of illustrations. Illustrations are a matter best taken up fully when you have written much of the book, for only then will you really know what kinds of illustrations and how many you might like to use, and be able to relate the costs of illustrations to their desirability for the book. Unless you are doing a heavily illustrated book, of course; then you will probably need some very special picture research and design help right from the start. If you are inexperienced, do not attempt to do a heavily illustrated book by yourself; the pitfalls are enormous. For other books, however, this is the time to make a preliminary assessment of what you will want, keeping your eyes open for likely illustrations as you research the work.

Seeking Outside Advice

Inexperienced authors, and many experienced authors as well, will usually find it useful to consult one or more professional editors as they develop a book idea into a book blueprint and sample. (We will discuss later what to look for in an editor and where to find such professional help.) The money you may spend on getting a sound evaluation of your projected work can be an excellent investment—possibly the most important investment you can make all during the publishing process.

Let us stress that such an evaluation is best secured from an experienced editor, even though it must be paid for, rather than from well-meaning friends and family. You should not expect competent evaluations from other authors or from local English teachers unless they are also experienced book editors. It is also wise to avoid agents who advertise such evaluations for fees, with the fee to be refunded out of royalty advances if the agent agrees to represent your book and then places it with a publisher. In these situations, the quality of the evaluation tendered must inevitably be suspect. Even more suspect is the kind of evaluation offered by a vanity publisher, who may tell you that your work is eminently publishable in order to secure a profitable contract to do your book. Get a reputable, tough, helpful editor early. Real help is what you need, not misleading, ego-satisfying self-interested bad advice.

With or without the help of an experienced editor, it is critically important in this early period to work and rework the idea, outline, and sample material, building an increasingly clearer view of your projected book—and then to pause, for as long as seems right, to make a thoroughly informed decision about whether or not to go ahead and write the book.

Beware momentum at this point. Momentum can help enormously once the decision is made and you are actually writing the book, but it can lead you into enormous error when you are trying to make a rational go-or-no-go decision. To put it as plainly as possible, most writers develop real affection for their own ideas after they have worked on them for a while. That is true even if those ideas are half-baked and the book is unfeasible. Publishers, in pursuit of their own economic interests, often shortcircuit poorly conceived books (though their works are not all well-conceived).

But writers who become author-publishers have no such built-in governors for their book projects; they are often perfectly capable of blinding themselves to problems and going ahead to write and publish when they should not.

One other element can affect the self-publishing decision. As we discuss in more detail later in this chapter, if the content of your projected book raises any questions at all—in anybody's mind—as to possible libel or invasion of privacy, that question should be checked out with an experienced lawyer before you make your self-publishing decision. If the book deals with contemporary themes, live people, or situations that can be construed to involve people now living, you may have such a question. For example, you would not want to do a book on a recent court case or political scandal without consulting a lawyer. Nor would you want to lightly undertake a work of fiction that—even quite accidentally—deals with people and situations that can be seen by a court as dealing in sketchily hidden form with living people, and which might be found to be libelous or invasive of privacy. Where the question exists, legal advice is essential, for the risks are very great.

But in the end, after all the preparation and advice, the self-publishing decision is always ultimately yours. The idea, outline, and sample material praised by so many people—including a good professional editor—may turn out badly. Or it may turn out rather well but find itself competing in the marketplace with ten other books on precisely the same subject, none of which existed when you started your book. On the other hand, the book everyone thought you quite insane to do may turn out to be an excellent piece of work, or a bestseller—or both, though that is even more unusual. The author as publisher is, of necessity, an entrepreneur, and self-publishing decisions are almost always very lonely ones.

At this point, you can still go on to one or more publishers, developed materials in hand, with or without an agent, attempting to secure a contract and an advance against royalties. What you have really done so far is to develop the kind of full presentation you would be likely to create if you were taking that standard route. Even during and after the period in which you are writing the book, you can continue to seek a publisher. The final self-publishing decision need not be made until the day you decide to fund production and marketing of the book, which can occur long after the writing has been completed. The decision to go ahead and write without a publishing contract implies a later self-publishing decision, though. Otherwise, you are simply writing a whole book on speculation—a well-worn path, but scarcely one experienced publishing people who cared about you would recommend.

Once you do decide to write your book, matters of personal style will determine how you go about it. Some writers take every chapter or section, hot off the typewriter in the roughest kind of draft form, and present it to one or more trusted editors and friends for comment, greatly valuing the resulting dialogue. At the other extreme, and far more often the case, very many writers cannot bear to have anyone else see what they are writing until they have finished the entire book, painfully worked and reworked it, and have an utterly clean final draft they consider the best they can possibly do.

If you can stand it, you may find it very helpful to pass your first few roughly drafted—but readable—chapters to an experienced editor for several kinds of comments. The possibility always exists that you will plan a book excellently, do fine sample material, and then tend to stray from planned content and writing style as you move into the book. A good editor—who knows what you are after, and is skilled enough to be able to help you realize your goals rather than try to impose his or her own style and goals upon your work—will help you check several such important matters early on. That kind of editor will check what you have done so far against your outline and sample, looking at such matters as content, length, clarity of expression, tone, and feel for the language, paying less attention at this point to such technical areas as grammar, usage, and spelling. Securing helpful professional comments two or three chapters into a book can be tremendously helpful for almost any writer. But if you find those kinds of comments at this stage too abrasive, just go ahead and write your book; the comments can come later.

Preparing the Manuscript

While this book is about self-publishing, not writing, there are some basic editing and publishing matters to bear in mind while you are writing your book. Whoever edits and composes your work, it will be best to observe a few standard rules on the mechanics of manuscript preparation:

★ Make sure that you work with a machine that will produce good, clean black print on paper. Use a good black ribbon on your typewriter and clean the keys as needed. Any machine with dirty type may produce e's that cannot be distinguished from o's, semicolons that may be colons, and commas that may be periods. Also be sure the type is clear; an old machine with worn type may produce print that is hard to read and therefore hard to edit and compose.

★ If you are using a word processor equipped with a dot matrix printer, be sure that the print is entirely legible, rather than faded and hard to read. Dot matrix printers vary considerably and some are very difficult to read, especially in large quantities as with a whole book manuscript. That makes editing and composing far more difficult and tedious than it should be, and leads to needless errors. Other widely used computer printer devices, such as the daisy wheel, will usually produce excellent copy for editing and composing.

★ Use paper with some opacity, body, and weight to it, rather than onionskin or other thin sheets. You need not use an expensive bond paper with substantial rag content. For manuscript purposes, the least expensive white, opaque, easy-handling, solid paper you can find is perfectly all right. That will probably be a 16- or 20-pound white paper without rag content that you will be able to purchase by the ream at any stationer's. To limit the "bounceback" of light that is so hard on the eyes, avoid papers that are too sharply white or too slick.

★ Editor and compositor should get a fully typed, double-spaced manuscript. Any handwriting in that manuscript should be limited to clearly printed minor corrections and changes put in during your own editing of the work.

Changes of more than a few words should be typed in; a change that will not fit above the line to which it refers should be typed on a separate sheet of paper and marked for insertion where you want it. Such long changes should not be squeezed into the margins, for that is hard on editors and not acceptable by most compositors.

★ Type on only one side of each piece of typing paper. Leave wide margins for editorial and composition purposes. About 1½ inches on all four sides is optimum.

★ Start each chapter on a separate page. Number your pages within each chapter as you go, with insert pages marked as "A" and "B" pages behind the page into which they will be inserted. That is for your own convenience as you work; otherwise, a chapter in progress blown about by an unexpected gust of wind, or absentmindedly scrambled by its author, may be very difficult to reconstruct. A dropped page can be missed for quite some time, with the rest reading quite plausibly.

When you pass your full manuscript along to an editor or compositor, though, be sure that the entire work is numbered consecutively, with any leftover internal numbering carefully crossed out. Standard publishing practice is to start numbering at the first page of the first chapter; but if the book is organized in parts, with a part page preceding chapter one, then you start by numbering the initial page of chapter one as page 2. Any material appearing before the part page or the first numbered page—that is all front matter—is numbered in lower case Roman numerals—i, ii, iii, iv, and so on.

★ Use standard copyediting marks throughout, when making corrections, additions, or any other kinds of changes on your manuscript. Editors and compositors can be thoroughly confused by nonstandard markings that may seem perfectly plain to you, but may convey entirely other meanings than you intended.

At the back of this book (see pp. 175-77) is a list of standard copyediting and proofreading marks commonly accepted by authors, editors, compositors, and printers. It is important to learn these publishing symbols and use them properly, as they are the physical means used by editors and authors as they pass a manuscript back and forth between them during the manuscript preparation process, and by editors to prepare a manuscript for composition. Whether you use a computer, employ a typist, or type your manuscript yourself—whether you, an editor you have retained, or a compositor marks your manuscript—someone ultimately will have to make the choices embodied in these marks and symbols. Whoever does this actually shapes the look of the pages of the book itself; if you want to have a hand in that shaping, you must at least understand what these marks mean, for to redo the design after composition is usually prohibitively expensive.

★ Indicate any quoted material clearly. Where the quotation is fairly long—certainly anything over one paragraph—set off the quote in a separate indented section without quotation marks.

Usage Questions

Beyond matters of manuscript preparation lies the whole area of usage, which also includes some elements of grammar and spelling. A standard style guide, a usage book, a good dictionary, and a thesaurus are musts for every writer—preferably more than one of each. These writer's tools are of the same order of importance as paper and ink. Two such style guides are *The Chicago Manual of Style* and *The New York Times Manual of Style and Usage*. You may also want to have one or more general usage books, such as Strunk and White's *The Elements of Style* and Fowler's *A Dictionary of Modern English Usage*. A writer should also have both a large unabridged dictionary, such as the Random House or Merriam-Webster dictionaries, and a substantial smaller desk dictionary, such as *The American Heritage Dictionary of the English Language*. For a thesaurus, an up-to-date Roget's is probably still most useful, though sometimes it is harder to use than might be expected.

One usage question that has not yet found its way into some generally sound usage books is the matter of desexing language, which has in the last decade become standard practice in modern writing, editing, and publishing. The writer or publisher who is insensitive in this area runs the considerable risk of being thought sexist by many readers of both sexes. It is wholly unnecessary and undesirable to trigger that reaction from reviewers and readers who might otherwise have been well satisfied with your work. Not all humans are male, and unless the "he" in your work is a specific person or a member of an all-male group, that "he" should probably be "he or she." On the other hand, a manuscript peppered with hers and shes and hims and hers can read rather awkwardly. The solution is more often to structure a paragraph so that the question does not come up, or to put the whole sentence in the plural, "they" being acceptably sex-neutral.

Manuscript Security

It is also vital to keep your manuscript physically safe while you are writing it. To see what may be years of work literally go up in smoke or float away in flood, when the only copy of a work is so destroyed, is one of the worst personal and professional disasters that can happen to any writer. No insurance can possibly cover the worth of such a lost manuscript. Even if there were such affordable insurance, the loss would still be irreparable, for notes and research—all the material that backed up the work—are generally lost at the same time. Nor is the work itself replaceable. Writers have written books once again after such a loss, but the second book is almost always a different book; the first book is gone, for very few of us have total recall.

Some writers keep fireproof boxes and safes, putting their work away every day as it is finished, and hoping that these devices will withstand fire, flood, earthquake, and theft. Others—and this is the course we recommend—make carbons of each page as they go, or print out second copies on their computers and deposit those carbons periodically in a safe deposit box or into the hands of a trusted friend who lives in a different place. There can still be a loss, but only of the most recent work. Most important, the likelihood of both copies being lost in the same disaster is very small. Relatively few writers properly protect their work in progress, by the way; those who do not are taking a statistically small but personally enormous risk. Every now and then, a newspaper story tells about the work of a painter, photographer or writer going up in flames. Painters cannot deposit copies elsewhere; photographers and writers can and should do so.

Writers who use word processors should not feel secure because their works are on discs rather than on paper. Discs are equally vulnerable, and it is wise to generate a second copy and store it elsewhere.

When working with typewriter and paper, you are likely to retype a page on which you have made very substantial changes, thereby generating a new carbon copy that can stored elsewhere. But when you work with a word processor, you are likely to make your changes directly on your computer, thereby changing the copy stored on your disc and making your disc one-of-a-kind once again. When that happens, it is wise to make a new "hard"—that is, print-on-paper—copy of the page, and put it in safe storage.

Word Processing: Opportunities and Hazards

Many writers feel that word processors offer excellent time- and cost-saving opportunities. Word-processing systems differ—that is one of the intrinsic problems connected with their use—but all have in common a keyboard, some kind of computer programmed to do editing and composition functions, a terminal that displays some portion of the material composed, and a printer.

In principal, such a system is similar to the kind of computer composition system used by compositors to set copy for publications. All that really differs is final use of the material composed. A computer-generated manuscript is said to have been produced by a word processor. The same manuscript translated into composed material ready for page makeup or printing is said to have been produced by a computer composition system.

Many writers and publishers place great emphasis on the savings possible when discs created on a writer's word processor are used to drive a composing machine, saving the second keyboarding traditionally needed when a copyedited manuscript is turned over to a compositor. So far, unfortunately, those savings have been somewhat elusive, as writers have found that the overwhelming majority of publishers use composing systems incompatible with the word-processing systems used by the writers to create their discs. In that case, the disc is simply used to produce print-on-paper copies, which are treated in the traditional way. Where publisher's and writer's systems are compatible, some of these possible savings have been realized.

The question of compatibility has been partially solved by translating devices between the different kinds of systems, as when copy is transmitted from disc to compositor over the telephone lines via a device called a modem. When savings have been realized, though, they have been savings for publishers rather than for writers. Indeed, some publishers have been supplying writers with instructions on how to mark their manuscripts for composition, expecting writers to do all their own editing, and refusing to share any of the savings with those writers. In essence, such publishers have been attempting to turn their writers into unpaid compositors as well—an attempt that is strongly and quite understandably resisted by most writers after initial fascination with computers has worn off.

For self-publishers, however, this area presents opportunity, as the question of exploitation does not arise. If an author-publisher likes writing with a word-processing system, has no problem with justifying the cost of such a system, and can either compose camera-ready copy using that system or solve the question of compatibility with compositors, some savings can indeed be realized.

While there are opportunities, there are also hazards with word-processing systems. Some physical writing and editorial problems are generally perceived; others are more obscure, especially to people in the first flush of computer-induced euphoria.

Writers using computers for long periods can encounter more eyestrain and more neckaches, backaches, and headaches than they did when using typewriters or working by hand. Some eyestrain is always associated with long hours spent looking at type on paper. That is true no matter how comfortable the typewriter, how easy-to-read the type, and however well chosen the paper. That many writers and editors tend to suffer eyestrain is simply a fact of life and a normal occupational hazard. But take one pair of already-tired eyes and glue them for many hours a day to a smallish screen with a good deal of light radiating from it; then tie that screen to a printer that prints gray type on grayish paper—and you have a recipe for ocular disease. When the screen and keyboard being used are not high enough off the floor and have insufficient leg room for easy use, you also have headaches, neckaches, and backaches on a grand scale.

If you are going to use a computer as a word processor, take great care to buy one with adequate leg room and a keyboard that is comfortable for you. Make sure that the screen is the most easily readable one available—and be prepared to switch to another, even more readable screen as soon as one can be found. Study the different printers available, and choose one that produces clearly readable type on easy-on-the-eyes paper. Above all, do not assume that you must settle for strain and inconvenience. If you can't find something you find really usable, don't buy anything at all. A poor computer setup can do a writer a great deal of avoidable physical harm.

Radiation hazard also may be associated with prolonged computer use. Much recent American research indicates that little or no hazard is associated with such use; but some American health researchers and many other health professionals around the world still express considerable reservations about computer radiation hazards. At the very least, pregnant women would be prudent to avoid prolonged computer radiation exposure. Beyond that elementary precaution, each writer will make an individual decision.

Many find writing with word processors greatly satisfying. And so it can be for some, as long as you take care to do a sound, structural, self-editing job as you go. Two potential problems are connected with self-editing on screen. The first is that as you work and self-edit on screen, you will lose prior—and often better—versions of your material. That is no great problem as regards the excision of typos, the correction of misspellings, the quick fixing of grammar, and the like. But it can be a very great problem indeed if you come to the end of a chapter with only the final version of that chapter in hand, on disc, having wiped away all previous versions and pieces of versions by correcting as you wrote. Most writers have felt the annoyance and wry relief that comes upon realizing that the first or second draft of a paragraph is better than the fifth. But if that first or second draft is not available—if it has been wiped away in a word processing system—there is no way to even compare it with later drafts. The cumbersome, inconvenient solution is to capture—in print or on disc depending on your system and how you work—each substantial piece you excise, so that you may reevaluate it as needed. The standard and quite correct advice for writers is to save every word they create; that applies to writing on computers as well, however they have to work it out technically. That means every draft, every page, every paragraph.

The second potential writing problem with word processors has to do with structure. People working on screen can have difficulty relating what they are writing to what they have previously written, even when they are working to outline. A piece of work has its own momentum. It changes as you write, developing internal

balances and problems and a life of its own that is always somewhat different from the work you had planned. When working with
print on paper, many writers go back and forth between pages,
sections, and chapters, comparing, balancing, and restructuring
as they go, doing the same with current and previous drafts.

Writers working with word processors must find ways to do the
same kinds of structural comparisons and reworkings as they go.
It could be done on several screens, using several identical discs
simultaneously—if the technology were available at affordable cost.
That may come, but it is not here yet and will not be soon. But at
the moment, the writer can do the necessary comparisons effectively only with print on paper; that is an additional reason for
saving everything you write—and probably on paper. Ultimately,
your book will be better for it.

Professional editors are meeting some rather difficult new problems with writers who have learned how to work on word processors
as effectively as they did on paper alone. Some rather experienced
writers are presenting editors with clean, seemingly errorless
manuscripts—right off their computer printers—that don't make
nearly as much sense as the funny-looking correction-laden manuscripts they used to produce. When an experienced writer using a
word processor produces a manuscript in which sections of the same
chapter do not quite follow each other, and pieces are repeated in
only slightly modified form from chapter to chapter, it is probable
that the author did not do a final, careful, old-fashioned print-on-
paper self-edit by hand. It is a must—and never more so than for
self-publishers.

Similar problems can be created by writers responding to editorial suggestions by rewriting portions of their manuscripts on their
computers. Receiving a freshly typed, entirely clean manuscript
back after correction and rewrite can be daunting and defeating
for an editor who is trying to be helpful as possible. Editors often
do not quite know whether or not a suggestion was accepted and
how it was acted upon without a very careful and time-consuming
comparison of drafts. A good editor, like a good writer, needs to be
able to trace the evolution of a piece of work, to compare the original version to the revision, and to back up and take a fresh look
when necessary. Editors and writers working with computers need

to find the way to create tracks they can follow together if their joint work is to be fruitful.

Working with Editors

At the end, a book really is a shared work if the editorial job has been a sound, committed one. The vanity publisher who does only a very light edit in pursuit of profit does an enormous disservice to a writer. So does the trusted friend, spouse, or former teacher "who just can't bear" to hurt a writer's feelings; however, without the requisite skills, they are not likely to do much good, no matter how frank they may be.

The amount of back-and-forth between writer and editor during the writing of a book is a matter of writer's preference. But after a manuscript is reasonably complete, self-publishing authors who do not seek competent editorial help run the risk of writing and publishing much poorer books than they have really written. An otherwise excellent book can be fatally afflicted by relatively minor and easily reparable defects of spelling, punctuation, grammar, and usage. And an author with a great deal to say and the ability to say it well can publish a mediocre book that could easily have been an excellent one had a skilled editor done the necessary deep structural work to make the book more comprehensible.

Yet very many self-published books are completed without skilled editorial help. Some are composed by their authors as they go, on word processors that effectively serve as manuscript composition machines, producing copy that need only be given to a compositor for composition directly from the author's disc. Most are given to a compositor in typed form, marked for composition by someone employed by the compositor, then composed and printed. Some good books are done this way, but not many. It is lack of skilled editorial help that makes so many self-published books much less than they might and should be, and marks them as amateur efforts.

For the relatively small expenditure of a few hundred dollars, a freelance copyeditor should be able to provide fairly light but effective treatment of spelling, punctuation, grammar, and usage. If your manuscript needs deeper editing, a good copyeditor will either be able to do the job or will be able to recommend someone who will. Whether early or late in the life of the work, the self-publishing author will be helped a great deal by working with a competent editor.

This does not mean that the editor should be given free rein. Writers have to be skeptical and to fight to make their own decisions as to what finally appears in their books. That having been said, the writer who stubbornly refuses relatively minor and much-needed alterations made by a competent editor is doing the work a disservice. It is almost impossible to see your own work clearly, especially after having labored long and lovingly over a book. Yet in the finest manuscript, much still needs to be changed. The key to success in this area is the choice of editor; you must find someone whose judgment you trust and whose approach to the work is compatible with yours. A good editor does not change meanings, but rather works hard to help the writer to clarify and enhance what has already been said. Nor does a good editor engage in destructive criticism or personalities; all that is unprofessional. And, contrary to even some publishing industry opinion, a fine editor certainly *does* mince words, putting the most devastating criticism in the most helpful, constructive way, with the easily damaged ego of the writer always in mind. No very good editor wants to win battles with authors; the aim of it all is to produce an excellent book that has been written by the author. Even if the book is being ghostwritten, the aim is to produce an excellent book that entirely represents the credited author's intents and understandings.

Arrangements for working with editors are loose and various, so there are no specific guidelines to follow. Freelance editors normally submit a bill on completion of work, receiving no payment in advance. You would be wise to have the editor look over your material first and give you a quick estimate of the anticipated amount of work and cost; then have the editor work on a small section of the material and submit it for a non-returnable fee. At that point, you and the editor can reasonably assess whether or not to continue working together for the balance of the project. If so, you would normally pay the editor the balance of the fee on completion of the work; if the work is a large one, you may want to stage both work and payments for control and fairness all around. If you and the editor are strangers, you may want to lay out the general terms of your agreement—what is to be done and the price or rate to be charged—in a letter. (No formal contract is usual in these situations.)

Arrangements for working with writers are similar, except that ghostwriters often participate in advances in commercial publishing situations, so would expect some sort of advance before beginning the work. Again, have the writer produce a sample, for a non-returnable fee (a "kill fee," paid even if the work is never used), to see if you are compatible before committing yourselves to the whole project.

Be sure to obtain a work-for-hire release from anyone who is writing or rewriting copy for you; work produced for hire is, under the 1978 copyright law, not automatically copyrighted in the name of the author, so this is—in essence—a waiver of rights in the material. Again, no standard form exists, but a paragraph like the following in a letter of agreement signed by both you and the other party should cover the situation adequately:

> Writing produced by you for (name of book) shall be considered a work made for me for hire, and I shall own the copyright and all of the rights comprised with the copyright. If this work does not qualify as a work made for hire, then you hereby transfer to me during the full terms of the copyright and all extensions thereof the full and exclusive right comprised in the copyright of the entire body of this material.

Be sure that some such letter of agreement is signed *before* any work is done; otherwise you may find yourself in the unhappy situation of a self-publisher who has paid for work but does not own the copyright.

Appendix 1, Sources of Information, is designed to help self-publishing authors reach into such professional publishing sources as *Literary Market Place* for expert help in editing and related areas.

Illustrations

Many kinds and levels of illustrations may characterize a book. Some books will be straight text. Others may carry only modest illustrations like a few tables and charts which may or may not have to be prepared by an artist, depending upon their complexity and your graphics skills. Some books will have a few photographs by the author, needing only placement in the book. Others may have dozens or even hundreds of photographs, woodcuts, drawings, and paintings, all or most of them requiring picture research, technical evaluation as to suitability for book production, and skilled placement into an intricately designed book. Whether the author-publisher will be able to handle illustrations alone or will need highly skilled professional research, evaluation, and design help depends entirely upon the needs created by the kind of book being done. The author-publisher whose work requires substantial illustrations but who is inexperienced in book illustration matters is quite likely to need expert help. In the long run, such help will probably save time and money, especially in the area of picture research.

Picture research is a whole sub-specialty in publishing. That is because needed illustrations can come from such a wide variety of sources all over the world, and can cost as little as a few cents or as much as $150–$200 for a single use in a book. A superb nineteenth-century woodcut, technically and in content exactly right for the book you are writing, may be available in a collection of out-of-copyright illustrations that costs only a few dollars, needing only to be cut up for use in your book. The cost of securing the illustrations will then be only the price of the book divided by the number of illustrations you take from it, possibly only a few cents per illustration. On the other hand, a current color photograph, in copyright, may cost $150 or even more to use, in the form of a fee to the copyright owner plus technical reproduction or rental fees. In between, there are a wide range of possible costs—and the need to find the kinds of illustrations you want at an affordable price.

One museum may supply you an excellent print of a work in their collection for only a $5–$10 technical and handling fee— probably less than it really costs them out-of-pocket to make and send the print to you. Another may see such prints as a source of much-needed income and charge you $50 plus technical and handling fees. For out-of-copyright illustrations in works that you cannot or do not wish to cut apart, you can hire a photographer or a local print shop to provide you with reproduction copy for $3–$15 apiece. A copyright holder may charge you $25 – $100 for a photoprint, a commercial photo supply house may charge more—but you may be able to get just as good a photo for your purposes from government and other public domain sources for as little as a $5 handling fee. You may even be able to get what you want entirely free from the public relations office of a corporation, labor union, or other similar institution. There are no easy general guidelines about when to obtain illustrations yourself and when to call in professional help. Indeed, sometimes it is wisest to do both, supplying what you can easily and inexpensively secure yourself and going to a professional for the harder-to-find illustrations. See the Sources of Information section at the back of the book for ways to start on picture research.

When you do secure illustrations yourself, be sure to consult someone who knows a good deal about pictures, print, and paper to assess whether or not the selected illustrations are suitable for reproduction in your book. That is a matter not simply of the sharpness of the print, but also of how each print will reproduce on your chosen book paper. In turn, your choice of paper greatly affects the production cost of your book; to secure good advice on illustrations can be vital.

An experienced book designer is your best advisor on this—the earlier the consultation the better, for the high costs of securing some kinds of illustrations and of producing a heavily illustrated book may deeply affect the entire course of writing, producing, and selling your books. At the most basic, you may not be able to afford to publish some kinds of heavily illustrated books. Even if you do have or can find the money to do so, you may ultimately decide not to for pricing and selling reasons. A heavily illustrated book, done in the short production runs that characterize most self-publishing, is usually a much more expensive book than a self-publisher can price low enough to sell at a profit. And priced too high, it may be hardly salable at all.

It is possible, however, to do a book that is quite satisfactorily illustrated at an affordable cost, and to be able to price and sell it profitably and in adequate quantity. Illustrations can be grouped, with perhaps a single 8–32-page group bound into the center of your book. Expensive-to-secure illustrations can, for many books, be replaced by equally suitable and far less expensive illustrations in the public domain—that is, works out of copyright or originated by Federal, state, and local governments, which, by law, cannot be copyrighted. You will probably want to do at least enough research in picture sources so you can talk with a skilled researcher intelligently and direct research efforts in the right directions. You will almost always want to work with a skilled book designer early enough to be able to make informed decisions as to the quality and quantity of the illustrations you will place in your book, so that you can make the right costing, publishing, and marketing decisions.

Libel and Invasion of Privacy

At this stage, also, you should review your work for potential libel or invasion of privacy problems. In a terribly litigious society, writers must be very much aware of the hazards created by lawsuits directed against them. Such lawsuits are now often initiated on what to many writers seem the flimsiest of bases; yet a lost libel or invasion of privacy suit—or, in some instances, even the legal costs connected with a *successful* defense against such a lawsuit—can mean financial ruin.

Let us be very clear that what follows here is not a treatise on copyright, libel, and invasion of privacy law. Far from it. Our aim is to provide only a most basic set of comments and to strongly urge you to behave most conservatively in these areas. It is not enough to have a good case that lawyers may win for you if somebody sues. What is necessary is to avoid having to hire lawyers to defend you. A large publisher figures in the cost of defending such lawsuits as part of the cost of doing business; a small self-publisher can be ruined by the legal costs attending defense of such a lawsuit, even if that defense is successful and the one who sues gains absolutely nothing from it. Nor can you depend upon a judge or jury to award you legal costs even if you win, so success here may not be success at all, but the worst kind of failure. The right question to ask a legal advisor in this area—and to ask yourself as well—is *not* "Can we win if somebody sues?" Rather, it is *"How can we do this so that the risk of any kind of suit is nil or negligible?"* The accompanying question must always be *"If somebody does sue, how much is it likely to cost us to defend the suit?"*

Libel and invasion of privacy matters form a whole field in the law; there are lawyers who spend most of their careers focusing on these kinds of cases. Here we can only review enough of the basics to make it possible for you to see when it is right to seek professional advice before potential problems become economically disabling ones, and to be able to communicate with lawyers working on such matters.

A *libel* is a published defamation of character, which may appear in written, broadcast, or pictured form, or in any other form except direct speech to others. (Defamation in the form of direct speech to others is *slander*.) The libelous statement must be false; must apply to an identifiable living person; and must be damaging to that person's reputation. Be careful here; so far, you are protected from actions based on alleged libel of the dead, but there is some possibility that the courts will change the law in this area in the future. And bear in mind that living survivors may be libelled by your writing, even when the main thrust of that writing is directed toward the dead. Also that by "person" the law really means any legal entity, including corporations and associations; these can survive long after the people you are writing about have died, and may in some instances bring suit against a writer. Such a suit may not be successful, and the lawyer who carries off your life savings after having successfully defended such a suit may have every reason to feel triumphant. But not you; you will have won only a pyrrhic victory.

The law of libel, while based on a single body of common law, differs somewhat from state to state, and what may not be libelous in one state may slip over into libel in another, as interpreted by the courts of that state. Note that although definitions often describe libel as "malicious defamation" and "malicious falsehood," the modern tendency in the United States has been to interpret the element of maliciousness almost out of the law of libel, except where public figures are involved. As a result, quite innocently intended writings may rather easily be judged libelous if they can be shown as false or unprovable, and damaging to the reputations of identifiable persons or organizations. Note that it may help to be able to prove that you did considerable research in good faith, consulting in the process a number of sources, but that this may not shield you entirely from a lawsuit, or for that matter a successful lawsuit against you. One rule that has for many years been followed by responsible journalists is the "three source rule," meaning that three independent sources have been consulted on a question of fact and all have agreed. Even that will not shield you entirely, but can help you to win or to suffer only smallish damages if you are sued. The problem of lawyers' fees will remain, though; it is by far best to try hard not to be sued at all.

Writers of fiction must be almost as careful as those writing nonfiction, checking city directories if they are using unusual names, taking care to use nonexistent addresses, and making very sure not to create and speak ill of fictional people who are too much like people with whom they have been associated or who have been in the public eye.

As regards living real people, the writer's potential problems include the question of *invasion of privacy,* which can also be actionable. Here, no defamation or malice need be present, or even alleged.

Like libel, this is by no means a settled area in the law—far from it. A great deal of the hazard here stems from the rapid development of electronic means of intrusion into the private lives of individuals, the epidemic use of those means by governments and media, and the insatiable appetite of the media and the public for information and news which may violate the right to privacy. As the pressures against privacy have grown, so have the reactions of individuals and courts, resulting in a widespread and often successful assertion of the right to privacy.

A good deal of current invasion of privacy law turns upon the question of whether or not someone whose privacy is allegedly invaded is a public figure, whether due to normal positioning in the public eye or temporary notoriety. A politician, actor, or athlete is likely to be seen as a public figure, as may be the defendant in a murder case. But the murder case defendant—or, for that matter, any of the others—may *not* be a public figure thirty years later when invasion of privacy is alleged. This is a very difficult area, and the law here changes rapidly as new court cases develop.

What is very clear is that writers can be vulnerable to invasion of privacy actions when they harass others, steal documents, engage in covert listening, enter homes when unauthorized to do so by use of deception, make unauthorized photographs and recordings, or similarly grossly intrude into the lives of living people. They are also vulnerable when they use people's names or likenesses without their consent, although this is mainly a matter of unauthorized commercial use rather than in matters of newsworthy or general interest, as when a photographer sells unauthorized pictures taken in the course of such invasion of privacy.

The main modern problems connected with alleged invasions of privacy by writers revolve around the publishing of facts about living people which those people view as private, embarrassing, and protectable from public scrutiny. The law is uncertain and the costs of defending against such a lawsuit can be enormous, even if you win. If you are writing about people, organizations, or matters that may raise libel or invasion of privacy questions, by all means have a lawyer experienced in these matters read your finished manuscript. If, right at the start, it is clear that such questions exist, discuss the projected work with an experienced lawyer before you start writing, so that you can avoid problems as you go; you may even decide not to proceed at all if the hazards are too great. These are sound procedures whether you are self-publishing or being published by another. You should not rely upon a publisher's lawyer to protect you, for their needs and yours may be very different. What is an acceptable risk of litigation cost to a large publisher may be a totally unacceptable risk to an author, whose contractual obligation to share the costs of defending lawsuits may become a ruinous burden.

Self-publishing authors should also insure themselves against libel and invasion of privacy actions. An increasing number of companies issue such insurance with reasonably affordable premiums. Some companies even routinely include libel—but not necessarily invasion of privacy—in their homeowner's liability insurance policies, as part of a quite inexpensive optional addition to standard general policies covering many kinds of potential liabilities. Should your broker not have an appropriate policy to offer, the Author's Guild should be able to supply the name of companies that do offer such coverage.

Permissions

All *permissions* to quote the work of others should be secured before the finally copyedited manuscript is put into composition. Where copyright holders are unwilling to grant requested permissions, or want permissions fees that are higher than you are willing to pay, you may want to write fresh copy in the place of the foregone quote, or otherwise adjust the copy so that the quotation is no longer needed. That is usually very easy to do in manuscript, but sometimes rather expensive to do after composition has begun. Don't merely paraphrase a quote; that can be seen as a copyright infringement.

When you do want to quote the work of others, the safest assumption to make is that you will have to secure written permission to do so, no matter how short the quote may be, unless the work being quoted is either uncopyrightable or out of copyright.

Uncopyrightable work is that which is financed directly with public money; that is, work published by a Federal, state, or local government organization of any kind. For example, a booklet on taxation written by government employees or by writers in the pay of the Internal Revenue Service or the Treasury Department is, by its nature, in the public domain; it cannot be copyrighted, and can be quoted from or, for that matter, used whole by you or anyone else who wishes to do so. The same is true for a booklet on local history issued by a city or county government, or a book on personal health issued by a government agency of any kind. That includes illustrations; for example, the Works Progress Administration (WPA) photographs of the 1930s continue to be a wonderful source of excellent illustrations for generation after generation of authors and picture researchers. Do be careful, though, about copyrighted material included in government publications with attribution to the copyright holder. If you see that something included in a government publication is protected by copyright, then get permission to quote or otherwise use.

Out-of-copyright work is that which has been copyrighted, but has run through its copyright period. Until January 1, 1978, when the current copyright law went into effect, copyrights in the United States lasted for an initial period of 28 years, were renewable for 28 years more, and then ended, with the copyrighted work then going into the public domain. But for some years before the 1978 law went into effect, a series of extensions were grafted onto the law by Congress, with the first period remaining the same, but the renewal period steadily lengthening. With the new law in 1978, the standard extension or renewal period became 47 years. Therefore, when copyrights have not been renewed after the first 28 period, they have expired. But when they have been renewed, the total period has become 28 plus 47, a total of 75 years.

Some copyrights were not renewed after the first 28-year period; most were. Therefore, a proper working assumption is that all works published in the United States 75 years or more before publication of your work are in the public domain, including the illustrations. A book published in 1985 may therefore safely use work published in 1910 or earlier. As to work that was not renewed after its initial 28-year term, it is possible to check the annual Federal copyright register, which is available in some major libraries, or to query the Federal copyright office in Washington as to whether the work is in copyright.

How long a quotation must be before you need ask for permission to quote is quite unclear in this period. The law is in considerable conflict and flux in this area, and prudence is very much in order here. You may quote only a few words of a poem or song and need to get permission from the copyright owner. You may quote as little as a short sentence from a work of prose and need to get permission. On the other hand, you may quote a whole paragraph from a different work of prose—and appear before a different judge, in a different jurisdiction—and be judged safely in the area of "fair use" with permission unnecessary.

As a practical matter, though, defending a lawsuit for copyright infringement is likely to be far more expensive than any quote or combination of quotes you might want to use. It is true that, in most instances, the copyright owner will only demand payment when the unauthorized quote is discovered; on the other hand, a copyright owner can also refuse you permission to quote at all and, if that occurs after your book is published, can force withdrawal of your book.

When you want to use a quotation, ask for permission. Pay no attention at all to those who advise you to quote without permission because your quote is brief or because the quote is likely to slip by unperceived by the copyright owner. In very practical terms, it is wise for the self-publishing author to ask for permission to quote anything in copyright and to behave as if, in this context, the doctrine of "fair use" did not exist, when quoting anything more than a phrase or very short sentence from a work of prose, and to ask for permission for anything at all quoted from a work of poetry or song. It is also wise to acknowledge the source of any quote or paraphrased quote you use, whether or not you have asked permission to use it, to avoid any possibility of charges of plagiarism; also to keep careful records of all permission requests and responses.

Here is a sample permission letter. Note that it should include basic publishing information about your book, including the intended market, and the size of your first printing. You are best advised to ask for English language world rights; if you later want to sell your book to non-English-speaking countries, you can always request permission for those rights. You will receive a form to fill out from some publishers, in addition to your permissions letter.

Some permission will be granted for the asking, and with little or no charge, especially when you explain in your letter that you are a self-publishing author. Most academic publishers, for example, will waive permissions fees, or will ask for as little as $10 or perhaps a copy of the book, for a modest quotation. Some permissions, however, may cost as much as $50–$100 when they must be secured from profit-conscious commercial publishers for whom permissions are viewed as part of a subsidiary rights "profit center." That is one reason to seek permissions as soon as you are quite sure that you are going to use them, right after the completion of manuscript and before copyediting. A high fee may cause you to reconsider use and change the manuscript accordingly.

You also may find that some desired permissions are hard and even impossible to secure, not because of cost, but because the copyright holder is inaccessible. Most publishing contracts provide for reversion of rights to authors when a book goes out of print. When that has happened, and many years ago, finding the author-copyright owner can become extraordinarily difficult. Publishers may not have former author's current addresses or may themselves have gone out of business, so your letters may reach no one who can grant permission. When that happens, and you are sure the work you want to quote is in copyright, it may be wise to change

(date)

Permissions Department
Penguin Books
40 West 23rd Street
New York, New York 10010

Ladies and Gentlemen:

I would like your permission to use a quotation from
Ronald Latham's translation of Marco Polo's *The
Travels,* published by you in 1958. A copy of the page is
enclosed, edited as it would appear.

The book in which I would like to use the quotation is
tentatively titled TO THE ENDS OF THE EARTH: THE
GREAT TRAVEL AND TRADE ROUTES OF HUMAN
HISTORY, to be published by Facts On File, Inc., in the
fall of 19___. The book will have a first printing of
approximately 0,000 copies, and will have mainly a
library sale, with some trade sale as well. We would like
world rights, English language. Because we are on a
short production schedule, I would appreciate an early
reply. If you have any questions on this, you can reach
me at 914-000-3333. Thank you.

Sincerely,

your plans, and not use the quote. On the other hand, if the quote
is central enough, you may want to take a modest risk and use the
quote, hoping that any aggrieved copyright holder who later appears will be satisfied by your show of due diligence in trying to
secure a permission and perhaps by a modest permissions payment.

Indexing

When the manuscript has been completed, copyedited, and is
ready for composition, nonfiction author-publishers can begin to
face the question of the *index.* Some nonfiction works, such as

dictionaries, may not require indexes, but most nonfiction is much enhanced by the presence of an adequate index, and is really quite incomplete without one.

There are basically two kinds of indexes. The first is a simple key-word index, which picks up those words and phrases you consider important and lists them in alphabetical order, with the pages on which they appear. You may do a single key-word index that includes all such words and phrases; or you may break out some sub-groups into separate indexes, as by subject, place name, and the names of persons included in your book.

The second kind of index is thematic, in which key words and phrases are grouped by subject or theme within the index. Because a single key word or phrase appears in several subject areas, such an index is considerably longer and more complex.

Indexing is very much a specialty in publishing, and an experienced indexer—such as one from the listings in *Literary Market Place*—is quite likely to produce a far better index than you will on your own, however careful you may be. The indexer will work directly from composed pages after composition and page numbering are completed, as that is by far the most efficient way to proceed. If you identify key words and phrases before pages have been numbered, you then must go back and attach numbers to those words and phrases when final page numbers become available. But if you wait until numbering is done, indexing can be done as a single unified process. The indexer is likely to charge you $1–$2 per composed page of your book, so an index for a 250-page book (roughly a 400-page manuscript), would run $250–$500.

You can do the index yourself, as very many self-publishing authors do, especially if you plan to include only one or more simple key-word indexes. Having a professional indexer in to do your index is not as centrally important as working with an experienced editor, and many an author has chosen to save money by doing the index even though the result will be not as good.

If you do the index yourself, you may be wise not to wait until you have composed pages, even though starting earlier is somewhat less efficient. Most inexperienced author-indexers need more time to think about what key words and phrases to include then do professional indexers. You can start identifying index entries after completion of the copyedited manuscript, and then have enough time to think over and revise entries while the book is being composed. Then when numbered pages are in hand, you can run through your entries and attach page numbers to them, using that numbering pass as a final edit of your index entries.

The Elements of the Book

Your book will also include several other elements. Here is an outline of the usual parts of the book, roughly in standard order. Not all of these parts will appear in each book, or in this order, but many books will have all or almost all of them.

First are the group of parts collectively called *front matter,* or *preliminary matter,* consisting of all those elements of the book preceding the main text.

Title page. In manuscript, this is a single title page that includes title and author. In the printed work a "half title" page, which is a page carrying the title only, will often start the book followed by a blank page, and then a full title page, which carries title, author, and the name of the firm you have formed to self-publish your book.

Copyright and related information page. This includes a statement of copyright; any further language aimed at protecting copyright; country of printing; Library of Congress Cataloging In Publication Data, if you have that information; International Standard Book Number (ISBN), if you have one; and identification of the edition and printing of your book. That is all standard publishing information. Self-publishers should also include the publishing or distribution address from which additional copies may be ordered. It is probably unwise to include price here, as you may want to change prices at some point, which is easy to do with a sticker on the cover but hard to do on the copyright page. The above information will all appear in the finally printed book; it will not be included in the manuscript you move from editor to compositor. As we later discuss, some of this information will be secured further on in the publishing process.

Dedication page. Usually appearing on a separate page, before the Table of Contents. This can be as brief as "To Ed" or a slightly fuller statement honoring one or more people. If you have one, keep it short and simple.

Contents. This is a section headed Contents, carrying numbered chapter titles and corresponding book pages. Take care to conform your final table of contents with the actual titles of your chapters, which may have changed during editing. Your printer will place actual page numbers on the title page after the body of the printed book has been paginated—that is, has received final page numbers.

Lists of tables, maps, and illustrations. This is sometimes a single mixed list and sometimes two or more separate lists. How to handle these optional parts depends on the number, role, and importance of these items in your book and is a matter of author's choice. These kinds of lists may be placed following the main text of the book, in the back matter, along with the index, but are more often carried as front matter.

Foreword. This is a relatively brief piece about the book, written by someone other than its author, usually as an implied or overt recommendation of the book by someone whose recommendation is thought to have weight in the book's field. The foreword should carry its author's name and credentials, if appropriate.

Preface. This is your own brief statement about your purposes in writing the book and, if you wish, how you went about the research and writing processes.

Acknowledgments. Here is where you thank all those who have helped during the course of your work on the book, either by name or as part of a more generally thanked group. Acknowledgments can very often be included as part of the preface without any kind of separate heading. It is wise to thank as many of those who helped as you reasonably can; the mystique of the printed book is such that those who are thanked often treasure that acknowledgment inordinately, and those who are passed over can resent your seeming neglect for a lifetime. Credit lines for quotations quoted by permission and for illustrations may be included in this section if they are not too numerous. Otherwise, they may appear in a separate section; sometimes with permission notices in the front matter and illustration credits in the back matter.

Introduction. This section begins to state the contents of the book itself, often outlining the main theses of a nonfiction work. As such, it usually is wiser to omit this section, placing this material directly into Chapter One, where readers will be less likely to skip over it.

Next comes the main body of your book or *text,* which may consist of these elements:

Part pages. If you have divided the several chapters of your book into parts, each consisting of several chapters, the main body of the book will start with a title page for Part One, carrying the part number and the title of the part.

Chapters. These are the main form of organization, each with its own title and covering a reasonably coherent body of material. You cannot expect the material to fall into conveniently similar chapter lengths, but you can meld together related materials to form chapters of more than a few pages long. Except for some novels, consciously crafted as a series of brief episodes, there is hardly ever a good reason to produce a book consisting of forty chapters, each an average of five pages long. Yet such awkwardly short chapters are found—regrettably often in self-published books. The problem is often a compound of inexperience at editing together the elements of your own work, and inexperience in visualizing the in-print size of manuscript chapters done by typewriter. Two typewritten pages may become one printed page; when that happens, your ten-page chapter in manuscript becomes a too-short five-page chapter in print. A skilled editor will solve the problem in editing. If you choose to edit the work yourself, you should be sensitive to the problem and adjust your chapters accordingly.

For most nonfiction, many authors and editors will want to break up the materials in chapters, for ease of reading, by inserting one or more ranks of *subheads,* which in essence serve as an extended outline of the work. In some kinds of books, as in some lawbooks, *footnotes* may be carried at the bottom of the pages, but this is an older style that is now seldom used. Footnotes are now usually r-ried as back matter, normally in sections corresponding to the chapters in which they appear; occasionally they are grouped at the end of each chapter. Sometimes, when there are very few footnotes in a whole book, it is easiest to carry them directly on the pages at which they occur, or in a single brief numbered listing in back matter.

Following the main body of the book comes its *back matter,* also called *end matter.* This matter, like front matter, is identified only by where it is placed in each book, that placement being wholly a matter of writing and editorial judgment. A glossary of terms or an index placed in the back of the book is back matter; the same glossary or index in front is front matter. Back matter may include:

A glossary of terms. This section defines and sometimes further explains some of the main and, perhaps, unfamiliar special terms used in the book.

One or more appendixes. These may include such materials as tables, charts, statutes, regulations and a wide variety of other supporting and informative material. Valuable material is often placed in appendixes to avoid interruption of narrative flow or because inclusion in place might unbalance the book. The same material could, in many instances, be set in place in the main body of the book; placing it at the back of the book is a matter of author's choice.

Lists of tables, maps, and illustrations. These may go in front or back matter, as we have discussed.

Footnotes. These may go in place, at chapter ends, or in the back of the book, as we have discussed.

Bibliography. This may be called "Additional Reading," "Further Reading," or by any similar name that identifies it as a list of other writings relevant to the contents of the book.

One or more indexes. As we have discussed, these are usually at the end of back matter but, in some kinds of reference books, may be placed into front matter for ease of use.

A colophon. This is a list of facts relating to the book itself, which in essence functions as a combined summary of production information and list of credits to those production craftspeople and artists who have worked on your book, including the printer, compositor, and designer. Your printer will usually be pleased to set this up in proper style for you.

All back matter, except for the index, should be completed as part of the book manuscript, including any bibliographic material you wish to include. Some of these back matter materials will also be covered in your index, as when a glossary of terms is included as back matter with the terms also picked up in your index.

Copyright and Related Matters

After manuscript completion, several editorial-related matters must still be done. All are easy to accomplish, though some may require a certain amount of time spent in filling out forms and passing paper back and forth between author-publisher and several government and book industry institutions. These include copyright registration, Library of Congress registration, the securing of an International Standard Book Number (ISBN), and completion of listing forms so that your book will be entered in *Books in Print* and in pre-publication book industry listings. None of these but the copyright registration is absolutely necessary, but all are worth doing, as they make your book easy to find for those who might want to order, examine, or review it.

As established by the 1978 copyright law, *copyright* exists as soon as you write your material. Not finish it; write it. Every sentence you write is copyrighted as soon as you create it. That does not absolve you of the need to register your copyright on publication of your book; that registration is a vital and conclusive element of proof that the copyright belongs to you. But it does remove a considerable hazard that existed under the old copyright law, as to the possible stealing of your work by others before copyright was effected.

Copyright protection starts as soon as you write a line of work, and continues for your lifetime and fifty years after. For works done anonymously or using a pseudonym, protection is for seventy-five years from publication or a hundred years from creation, whichever is less. Although the letter of the law states that you are protected as soon as you write a work, as a practical matter it is a must to state on your work that you are the copyright owner and to register published work with the copyright office. The current copyright law is still brand new, as these things go, having been in effect only since January 1, 1978, so almost all of its many quite unclear aspects have yet to be adjudicated, meaning that authors should bend over backwards to protect themselves. As self-publisher you should register your copyright yourself. That is easy to accomplish, and the copyright office will assist you if your registration form is improperly prepared.

Your copyright can be protected on the articles and books you write, as long as you do not create those writings as part of your duties while employed by another or sign away your rights by signing a "work for hire" document that gives away your rights in specific works done for pay as an independent contractor. You can also be copyright protected on other created works, including photographs, paintings, sculptures, other graphics, plays, musical works, works created for the dance, motion pictures in their several screen forms, audio recordings, and a miscellany of other audio and visual works.

The first step in claiming copyright ownership is to print that claim on the copyright page of your book, including the symbol ©, the year in which the copyright is being claimed, and your name or the name of your company as copyright owner, as in "© 1984 by Mary Smith."

You can obtain copyright form TX, which is the right form for books other than books of drama, from the Information and Publication Section, Copyright Office, Library of Congress, Washington, D.C. 20559.

When your book is printed, send the completed form, two copies of the book, and a $10 check payable to Register of Copyrights to: Register of Copyrights, Library of Congress, Washington, D.C.

20559. If you choose to register an unpublished work, all is the same, except that you need send only one copy of the work.

It is wise to send the application, books, and check to the Register of Copyrights within the first three months after publication, to ensure the best possible protection of your copyright, even though the work is by law copyrighted when you write it.

Before January 1, 1978, the copyright law penalized errors in copyright registration very heavily, sometimes operating to destroy copyrights in instances of defective registration. That is no longer so, and errors in registration can be corrected, but errors uncorrected for several years may cause damage to or loss of copyright protection.

Just as you may not take very much of the work of others without securing "permission," so others may not take your work. If your work is used without your written permission, your copyright may have been infringed upon. Sometimes that is obvious, as when large pieces of your work are used whole or in very lightly disguised form. More often, the infringement is not so large or so clear; then it is time to consult an experienced lawyer as to whether or not infringement has, in that lawyer's opinion, occurred; what it would cost to mount a case against the alleged infringer; and whether or not it might be worthwhile in an economic or personal sense to do so. Occasionally, as when someone really uses large quantities of your work, you can somehow justify the cost of what is bound to be a very expensive action. Usually, you cannot.

Library of Congress. Cataloging in Publication (CIP) data is an entry prepared for your book which allows libraries and other bookbuyers all over the world to catalog and easily order your book, functioning as a central source of information on forthcoming books. Relatively few libraries will order a book by an unknown author on the basis of simple notification via Library of Congress catalog cards. Some may, when a special interest book fits their own interests. For most, it is a useful convenience, when ordering your book, because of such reasons as review attention and library user requests. You can get the appropriate form to fill out by writing to the CIP Office, Library of Congress, Washington, D.C. 20540. Be sure to do so before publication of your book, so you can place the entry on your copyright page under the copyright notice. There is no charge for this registration, but an advance copy of your book should be sent to the CIP office as soon as it is available, and before the official publication date, so that cataloging may proceed.

The International Standard Book Number (ISBN) is a unique number assigned to your book, as an identification and ordering device. It is issued by the International Book Numbering Agency, at 1180 Avenue of the Americas, New York, New York 10036, which will send you the appropriate registration form. This is an optional but useful and easy-to-accomplish registration. It must be done before publication so that you may place the number on the copyright page of the book, generally under the Library of Congress CIP information.

The Advance Book Information (ABI) form is secured by writing to ABI Department, R. R. Bowker Company, 205 East 42nd Street, New York, New York 10017. This is a very important form to fill out and return early, because it generates not only a listing in *Forthcoming Books In Print,* which alerts pre-publication buyers to your book's existence, but also a listing in *Books In Print,* which is by far the most important information and ordering source used in the book trade. When someone comes into a bookstore seeking your book, but does not have your publishing address or the price of the book, the ultimate source to which the bookstore turns is *Books In Print.* Without a listing there, it is possible to lose many sales, especially if you are an unknown self-publisher.

Fill out the ABI form very carefully, describing your book and its author as fully and favorably as you possibly can, and casting its audience and subject appeal as widely as possible. Your book is going to be indexed in *Books In Print* and perhaps in several other Bowker publications. The better you treat it in the ABI form, the better it will be treated by the Bowker publications.

There is no charge for the ABI listing. Be sure to send it in six to nine months before your anticipated publication date, so that people who might want to do pre-publication reviews will not be put off by thinking the book is already in print. Be careful, by the way, to set your "publication date" six weeks to three months after you reasonably anticipate that your book will be off the press, partly to allow for pre-publication reviews, if any, and partly to allow enough time for shipment from the printer to those bookstores that have ordered them before your main promotion efforts are in full swing.

To complete these processes, once your book is in hand, you will want to send two finished copies to the Register of Copyrights to complete your copyright registration. You will also then be sending out your review copies, which may for some kinds of works run well over one hundred books. You should also then send one copy to the Library of Congress, one copy to H. W. Wilson's Cumulative Book Index (at 950 University Avenue, Bronx, N.Y. 10452), and one copy to *Publishers Weekly,* for listing in their *Weekly Record;* there are no charges for these listings.

CHAPTER 5

───────── ☆ ─────────

Design, Composition, and Production

A manuscript is one thing; a book is quite another. The author creates the manuscript; but to create a book, the author must develop the skills of a publisher.

As a self-publisher, you must first understand the main elements and choices involved. As every experienced publisher knows, hiring skilled people is not enough; you must be able to speak with those people intelligently about every aspect of book preparation, production, marketing, and distribution. And if you choose not to hire professionals to perform some of these functions, you must go beyond that, to develop the ability to work the elements and choices yourself.

When you write a book, planning and outlining as previously discussed, you are in essence conceiving and examining the book idea whole and then moving to outline it whole, all the while knowing that it will change a good deal as you actually write the manuscript.

With your publisher's hat on, you should take a similar approach to creating the book. You must first consider it whole with only manuscript in hand, and then examine and develop each element within the context of the whole book you have conceived. Do not confuse the publishing function with the design and production functions, which need to be directed by the publisher. That is why designer, compositor, and printer will look to you for direction, no matter how skilled they may be, and will undertake publishing functions only if it is clearly understood that they should.

The Physical Book

First, then, the book as a whole, starting with a very basic question: what kind of book do you literally, physically, want to see, to hold in your hand at the end of the publishing process?

A basic question, perhaps, but not necessarily a simple one to answer clearly, as your answer is likely to be constructed out of your answers to several related questions. All of the esthetic, functional, and economic choices discussed in Chapter 3—all the matters relating to audiences, funding, marketing, and personal goals—must be examined together when you are trying to decide what kind of book you eventually want to hold in your hand. One self-publishing author may be delighted with a smallish trade paperback, capable of reaching large popular audiences and perhaps making a good deal of money if it is well received. Another may feel the need for a big, hardcover book printed on high-quality, high-cost paper, to be sold at a high price to a narrow, but very receptive professional audience; such a book may enhance reputation and need not do much better than break even to be entirely satisfactory. Yet another will be satisfied with modest sales and modest financial losses, as long as the book is published and is, in the author's eyes, a physically beautiful book.

In physical terms, a book is composed of print and sometimes illustrations on material, usually paper, which is joined by glue or stitching and encased in a cover, which itself may have another cover, or jacket. If properly designed, all the elements of the book complement each other, and the internal design of each element works within the whole book design. A well-designed, light, bright, and airy children's book page design will work with a similarly designed cover; it will not work at all with a heavy, dark cover, which turns children and parents away so that they may not even open the book to see what is inside. At the other end of the publishing spectrum, a strong reference book that should appeal to serious information interests will not work very well if the visual elements overwhelm the reference content and therefore the usefulness of the work. Design follows publisher's perception of probable audience.

The easiest—and probably the best—way for a neophyte author-publisher—or, for that matter, one who has done several books—to proceed with book design, is to look for models or partial models and seek to work from them. That is really what most publishers do when they "see" their books early on in the publishing process. Publishers are not professional book designers who build books from the raw materials of book design; publishers are people who look at books they and others have done, and say or think, "I want something like that one over there."

If you want to design your own self-published book, or want to be able to intelligently direct the work of others in designing your book, go to the library and look at books, hundreds of books. Handle them. Look at their dust jackets, their bindings, the ways their contents are glued and stitched together, their page designs, type sizes and styles, the way the paper used holds inks, reproduces illustrations, and bulks up the contents of the book. Go to bookstores, and see how different book sizes and cover designs stand out on the shelf from across the store—and what designs, sizes, and cover color combinations fade away and are unreadable from any distance.

Read about what makes a book. Buy or borrow Marshall Lee's *Bookmaking: The Illustrated Guide to Design/Production/Editing*, the second edition of which was published by R. R. Bowker in 1979. It is an excellent book, made for professionals but written simply enough for non-professionals to understand well; and it is especially useful in the design and production areas. Bear in mind only that computer-composition technology is changing so quickly that the possible value of home-computer composition for self-publishers may seem underestimated.

Most of all, though, take other books in hand and see them and all their key elements *physically*. Then you will be able to develop the kind of feel for books and their physical elements that will enable you to work with designers, compositors, and printers to make good-looking books that accurately reflect your publishing desires.

Composition

Whatever mode of composition you use, the net effect of it will be the imposition of ink on paper, as it is on this page. Let us, then, separate the question of how to compose—and at what cost—from the question of how to make that ink on paper best suit your publishing desires and treat those desires first.

A whole web of esthetic considerations surrounds the question of which type to use on what paper; that is some of the main stuff of the type and book designer's art. And art it is. Each book is also an artwork, designed and produced by artists, no matter how well or ill artistic intentions are realized—or are even considered by those who made the book. In this sense, the writer is only the first among many artists who work together to produce the finished book.

But underneath artistic considerations are some basic assumptions, which have to do with effectively communicating the content of a book to its intended audiences. At its most basic, then, a book must be set in type that:

- is large enough to be easily read,
- lays flat upon the page being read,
- is printed in ink dark enough to be easily seen,
- has enough body to be easily seen,
- and is laid not too densely upon the page, so the eye can easily follow its flow.

How large a book type must be to be easily read is a somewhat subjective estimate. At the turn of the century, average book type sizes were considerably smaller than those generally acceptable by book designers and readers today. Yet even today, many newspapers use type sizes that are much smaller than most book types, as do many mass market paperback books and some reference books. What is probably safest is to use a type size similar to those used in modern hardcovered or trade paperback books, as that is what is likely to feel most acceptable to your audience.

Selecting Type

American type sizes are measured in *points*, with each point measuring vertically about 1/72 of an inch. For ease of reading, types measuring one size vertically are usually set into lines measuring vertically one or two points larger; this allows more space, or "air," between each line than if the type were set "solid" into a line of its own size. It is the vertical measurement that is used to describe size; the horizontal measurement varies with spacing and type style, and is not used for measurement purposes. Therefore, a type measuring 10 points high on a line 12 points high—described as "ten on twelve," and written 10/12—is 10/72" high set into a line 12/72" high. This is a very common hardcover and trade paperback book type size; the other two most common are 11/13 and 12/14. The page you are reading is set 10/12, in a rather readable type Century Schoolbook, which has adequate body for ease of reading, as well.

Some books carry their design specifications, usually in the back of the book, but sometimes in front matter. Unfortunately, that is an older style, which has fallen into disuse. But if you do find a book you wish to use as a model for your own, by all means show it to your designer, compositor, and printer. They will be able to measure sizes, recognize styles, and either duplicate or approximate those aspects that especially appeal to you—or tell you why they think those aspects inappropriate for your book.

Types come in families, usually named after their originators or early users, but sometimes after their style variances. (A specimen sheet of some common book types is given in Appendix 4.) The widely used Bodoni family of modern book typefaces, for example, is a modern Roman group, named after its originator; Times Roman is another good-looking and much-used family of typefaces. You will not go very wrong—and probably will go quite right—if you select a type of appropriate size out of one of these two families. Caution: beware the trendy designer who urges you to use an unusual and hard-to-read type that is the "coming" thing; it is usually just a fad. If you find a book type hard to read, trust your common sense and use something else. If you are unwilling to trust your common sense, seek other professional opinions, and ask other nonprofessionals if they too find the type hard to read. Whatever responses you get, read a whole page, and perhaps two, before you decide whether or not a type is hard to read, set too small or too large, or set too solid on the page, with insufficient air. Many types that are very attractive for an advertisement, with short pieces of copy, are very wearing on the eyes, when used for full pages of text.

Type size must be carefully considered in another way, too. A

difference of a single "point" in the type size you use can make a
difference of many pages in your book. You can adjust page number to some extent with the page margins you use, but can go only
so far before the book page begins to look cramped or, at the other
extreme, "padded" with too much white space on the page. The
main adjusting device is line size. A 6"x9" book set with 14-point
lines, rather than 13-point lines—a difference of just one point
vertically—and otherwise similarly designed, can have as much
as 15 to 20 percent more pages. That is because the difference vertically amounts to only a few lines per page, but the difference
horizontally is at least equally large; more characters fit into the
smaller-point line.

This question of the number of pages in your book can be of considerable importance. More pages mean higher paper costs, and
often higher total composition costs. On the other hand, more pages
can mean the difference between a small, credible book, and a book
that seems to its readers considerably too short to be called a full
book. A 60,000-word book in the hands of an amateur can become
a 100-page, fairly readable, but quite too small book. In the hands
of a sound professional, the same book can and should be an attractive, readable book in which the number of pages does not call
into question the substance of the book. The difference between
the two books is all in the type sizes, type styles, margins, and
trim sizes chosen. The 100-page book may be set 10/12, with small
margins and a 7"x10" trim size, the result being quite readable—
but far too small. The credible book may be set 10/12, 11/13, or
12/14, with largish, but not too large margins, and in a standard
small hardcover or trade paperback 5¼"x8" trim size; it might run
anywhere from 224 to 296 pages, depending on what combination
of type, margins, and trim size you choose.

The question of margins has another side, too. All too often, books
are set with too-small margins on the gutter, which is the inside
edge of the page. The page looks all right when it is laid out flat in
page proofs, before binding. But binding uses up some of the inside
margin, leaving the print squashed up against the binding and
making it hard to read. That becomes a particularly difficult problem when your book is a paperback with a "perfect"—that is, a glued
flatbacked—binding. Such books do not naturally lie flat, as hardcover books do. Instead, they open somewhat bent. If a reader must

flatten out a paperback book in order to properly read all the print on the page, that will inevitably break the back of the book. If you want your paperback book to be read easily and to survive its first few readings, be very sure to include ample gutter margins. For hardcover books, adequate gutter margins will suffice. And don't believe anyone who tells you that the new adhesives being used in books today have solved this problem. They are better adhesives than those previously used, but are not at all effective enough yet to solve the backbreaking problem of perfect-bound books. This is one of the key reasons that perfect-bound paperbacks are still intrinsically much inferior to books gathered in signatures, sewn, glued, fixed together and covered again with a back that allows them to be opened flat, the binding method used in hardcover and some flexibly bound books. We recommend that self-publishing authors seriously consider doing their books in trade paper—but only for economy, never for durability or readability.

Occasionally, a self-publishing author has the misfortune to run into a designer or printer who counsels the very "artistic" approach of using something like light brown ink on some kind of off-white or even bluish paper, or dark brown on light brown paper, or black ink on some other-than-white paper. You may even be shown how beautiful such a work can be—on a brochure, booklet, poster, or set of sample pages. Caution: don't do it. The reason that almost all books, including art books, in libraries and bookstores, are printed in black ink on white paper is that they are most readable that way. You can print lovely, unconventional, artistically interesting and satisfying books if you wish, but only with great care, in small runs, for very special audiences, and usually at a considerable financial loss, especially if you figure in your own time as art printer realistically. But that is art printing, which is quite different from the main-line self-publishing this book discusses.

The thickness of the body of a type considerably affects its readability. That is why typewriter type, which is quite acceptable and readable in relatively short newsletters and some kinds of advertising materials, is usually a bad book choice. The problem is that is too thin, and especially when reduced, or "shot down" from an 8½"x11" piece of typing paper to fit a smaller book page. It is very attractive from a cost point of view, certainly, being by far the least expensive way to set type, but for books it is better to use a composition mode that supplies a more standard, more readable book type.

Methods of Composition

From the compositor's point of view, there are now several modes of composition, all changing rapidly as applicable computer technology develops. From an author-publisher's point of view, however, there are three choices, which will change, but not essentially, with new technology. First, you can type—or have your book typed—on a typewriter and use the resulting manuscript as a set of composed pages from which plates can be made and a book printed. In this sense, typewriter composition is like any other kind of composition. There are special typewriters that will give you "justified," margins—that is, even margins both right and left on the page—if you wish, and will give you clean, even type from which entirely adequate printing plates can be made (with the reservation as to thinness previously expressed).

Second, you can type—or have your book typed—into a computer memory, create one or more discs containing your completed manuscript, and print it out on a printer attached to the computer, using one of the many word-processing systems and one of the several adequate small computers now available for these kinds of purposes. You need not own the computer; increasingly, independent typing services around the country are acquiring computer capability and developing their businesses into word-processing service centers. Some of those running word-processing centers now advertise in such professional sources as *Literary Market Place* and *Small Press*; as the practice spreads, others will become available through local advertising sources, such as local shopping journals and telephone directories. When you type your manuscript into your own computer, you are acting as your own primary compositor; when you hire a word processor to do it, you are, in essence, hiring a partial alternate to the traditional compositor. The word processor creates discs but does not yet have the equipment and skills to turn those discs into printing plates.

A computer-composed manuscript *can* produce a disc which can be used to create printing plates if it can be made compatible with available composition equipment. As we have previously discussed, that requires either finding a compositor who has compatible equipment or sending your disc's contents to the compositor through a modem which—to put it a bit over-simply but not inaccurately—strips your computer's formats from your manuscript and transmits the manuscript's information in a form capable of being taken by the compositor's computer and wrapped around with its formats. That is somewhat expensive as of this writing, especially if it has to be done over long-distance telephone lines. But that is less and less necessary as the new technology emerges, and the question of compatibility at a reasonable price between author-publisher and compositor computers is fast being solved.

Third, you can type—or have typed—your manuscript, make what corrections you wish, and hand your manuscript to a compositor. The compositor will use any of several methods to compose your book, most of them today (and all of them tomorrow) involving the use of computerized composition. From the author-publisher's point of view, this is rather a simple way to go about handling the matter; whether you do it this way or use computer composition yourself for a single self-published book will depend considerably upon whether or not you already have a computer, or have a computerized word-processing organization acceptably accessible.

Whichever of the three basic methods you use, there are some format and copy flow matters to take up at the composition stage. The term *format* can be a little difficult to deal with, at first. It really means every aspect of a publication's physical appearance, including such matters as type and type sizes, paper, bindings, and the many small choices that go into the final layout of a page. It is also commonly used to describe any single element of physical appearance and design, so that a compositor will be discussing and deciding "formats" with you at a time when you may not have even seriously considered the final specifics of paper and binding.

At the composition stage, the formats you will be deciding upon are those that determine how your book's content will lay in ink upon the pages of your book. That means type; page layout style; subheads within the text; how words are to break when carried over from one line to another; the indenting of paragraphs; how to head and start new chapters; whether to use running heads on the pages; how to handle the placement of illustrative material, tables, charts, graphs, and footnotes; how to handle bibliographic material; and quite a number of other such questions. All should really be decided before whoever is composing the book begins setting the main body of the book. All should be done by self-publishing authors in close consultation with hired professionals. This is the normal day-to-day stuff of a book designer's, compositor's, or printer's life; you should not expect to be able to master it all for a single self-published book, or even while doing several self-published books. And it is not simple; all the elements of design and resulting formats are interwoven.

That is, indeed, one of the little-recognized hazards for authors "composing" manuscripts on their home computer word processors. Each detail of the format must be specified and coded; for novices without professional guidance that can be an extremely difficult set of operations to perform with any success. Even for authors with strong editorial backgrounds, who are fully familiar with all the myriad of decisions that go to make up the format, coding those decisions into the text is still very difficult, as well as tedious and time-consuming. While such self-composing authors may save on out-of-pocket costs, the author's time is a significant expense in itself. And in some cases, so many changes must be made in the format that two composition passes are necessary—comparable to the two stages of galley proofs and page proofs in conventional composition—and the cost of the home-computer composition may represent, in the end, no saving over traditional methods. The only remaining advantage, then, is the speed at which the final composition stage is performed, and the ease of making small changes right up to the end of the process. For writers of timely works, as opposed to history or poetry, this can be a significant plus.

Before settling format questions, and no matter how skilled the people you have hired, you must see sample pages that embody all the format decisions you have made. It is an expense; sample pages may cost as much as a couple of hundred dollars. But there is no other way to really see how the pages and the several parts of your book will look. You may have chosen type that looked wonderful on a single line in a type specimen book and hate it when you see a whole page. You may have done a little thing, like accepting a recommendation that you indent paragraphs two characters only, in a commonly used modern mode—only to realize, when you see the page, that the choice here is quite wrong in terms of the appearance of the page. A two-character indent on a page of strong, readable type may make that page look as if it is almost a solid block of dauntingly unreadable type. Author-publishers, like all publishers, must lean upon the skills of many others—but the final publishing decisions are their own and must be fully informed.

However copy is composed, there is a certain amount of flow back and forth between author and compositor as final changes and corrections are made. Even if you compose your own copy, that is in a sense still so; if you fail to recognize this, because you are using a home computer as a composing word-processor, you run the real risk of turning out a book full of typographical errors. Actually, it is in one way more difficult to compose the book yourself, for you cannot see your own typographical errors as easily as others can. Your eye will slide over errors, even on a fifth rereading, while someone else is likely to pick up your overlooked errors on a first reading.

If you do your own composing, plan to print out your composed material and do a careful "author's read" of it. That will enable you to pick up some errors in content that may still remain, even after copyediting, and to make any final changes desired. Quite often, some final changes need to be made at this stage because situations or facts—or your view of a matter—have changed. Plan also to have someone else, preferably a skilled proofreader, do a final reading of your printed out manuscript for typographical errors. Some will inevitably slip through, as in every book, but not nearly as many as when you are content to do a final reading solely on your own and only on the computer screen.

Kinds of Proofs

If you compose through others, there will be some passing of composed material back and forth between author and compositor. Actually, what is passed is not the composed material, but rather copies of it, called *proofs*. "Proofs," like "formats," can be a little difficult to understand early on, and for much the same reasons. There are several kinds of proofs, all of them images of composed material, and most of them look quite alike to the author. Sometimes proofs are described by the stage of the production process at which they are made, as with *galley proofs, page proofs,* and *press proofs*; sometimes by who is going to use them, as with *author's proofs* and *reader's proofs*.

Galleys are long pages of composed type, set in a single column, which will later be put together with any other images, such as illustrations, that are to appear on a book page, and made up into pages. A *galley proof* is a copy of the composed galley on which you as author and other readers make changes and corrections. It is at this point, while you are reading the galleys, that some sets of uncorrected galleys may be bound and sent selectively for pre-publication reviews. The galley proofs are then returned to the compositor, who makes the changes indicated on the galleys themselves and then moves on to *page makeup.*

Alternatively, composition can be done directly into pages, bypassing the galley stage and saving some money. Before computer composition that was rarely done, as it was very expensive to make author's changes once pages were made up: to break up and remake large numbers of pages to accommodate new pieces of copy was prohibitively expensive. With computer composition, however, it has become possible to "push" type forward or backward within a computer memory; that makes changes at the page makeup stage much less expensive. With computer composition, the page is not physically made up until all changes have been made; before then, what changes is only the formatted copy in the computer's memory.

When you do use a compositor, it very much pays to give that compositor a clean, fully corrected manuscript to work from. Heavily edited, hard-to-read and hard-to-compose manuscript will be classified as *dirty copy,* sometimes called *foul copy*; it will both generate extra composition charges for being what is called *penalty copy* and cause many unnecessary and expensive composition errors.

In reading proofs at any stage, it also pays to carefully mark any typographical errors made by compositors as *PE,* which means *printer's error*; the compositor, not you, bears the cost of correcting these. Your compositor will, by agreement with you, allow you to make a certain amount of changes without additional charge; these are called *AAs,* meaning *author's alterations.* The usual agreement enables you to make changes up to about 10 percent of the cost of setting the original manuscript. Above that amount, you will be charged extra for author's alterations. Therefore, be sure to clearly mark printer's errors so that they will not be charged against your allowance for author's alterations. Note that a 10 percent author's alterations allowance does not mean that you can change 10 percent of the words in the manuscript without additional charges. Inserting changes can cost a good deal more than composing a body of copy word for word; your 10 percent cost allowance is likely to mean, in practice, that you should not plan to change more than 3 to 4 percent of the words in the manuscript without incurring extra charges. But you will be wise to keep your changes far below that, for they can introduce errors in the final stages. Do your editing in manuscript; in the proof stages, make vital changes only.

Page proofs are copies of composed, made-up pages, whether these are constructed from galleys and other material or are done directly. Any final changes are made on these proofs, and it is here that you can check to see that any changes and corrections put in at the galley stage were properly made. If you bypass galleys, you should arrange to have a second set of page proofs sent to you so you can do this final check. At the page proof stage, you can also, for the first time, get a full view of how the body of the book will really look. This is when any final content and design doubts will surface—but only if they must; major changes at this stage are very, very expensive.

Later on, when the pages of the book have been all made up into forms to be put on the printing press, your printer is likely to draw *press proofs* in order to take a final look at the book just before printing. If you are doing an art book, or a heavily illustrated work, you will want to look at those press proofs; even more likely, you will want your designer to study them carefully. Otherwise, it is probably unnecessary and may indeed be quite impractical if your book is being done as a short run in a remote location. Production schedules change; machines break down. It doesn't make much sense to travel from Detroit or Buffalo to a short-run printer in Ann Arbor to examine press proofs if you are not even sure those proofs will be there to examine when you arrive.

Your printer will also be checking *blueprints;* these are contact prints made from the films of your *mechanicals,* which are composed pages pasted up in final form to see how illustrations have photographed and are likely to print. As with press proofs, you need be involved with blueprints only if you are doing an art book or a heavily illustrated work. Blueprints can also be called brownprints, silver prints, vandykes, and several other names, depending upon the process used; for author-publisher purposes, you need only know that they all perform the same basic function.

Paper

Like any other publisher, you should seek a paper that most economically suits the content of the book and your aims. A paper suitable for an inexpensive newspaper that is destined to be thrown away shortly after purchase is entirely unsuitable for a book that is meant to last for decades. A paper quite suitable for a book composed entirely of print on paper may be quite unsuitable for a book composed largely of illustrations. A glossy paper that is wonderful for a highly illustrated book may be wholly inappropriate for an all-text work for the very reasons that make it good for illustration reproductions; the bounceback of light from a hard, very white, very glossy paper may be fine for light, airy copy, but almost impossible for the protracted reading of solid text.

Using other books as models may help you little in assessing suitability and price, for the book you choose from the library shelf may be made of paper far better and more expensive than anything you can reasonably buy today. Hidden inflation is the worsening of materials and workpersonship; it applies throughout the society, and to paper as much as anything else. Like commercial publishers, the self-publishing author needs expert buying help in this area. Publishers don't buy paper, their production departments do; publishers make buying choices within the range of possible papers suggested by skilled production people. Self-publishers should try to work similarly, often buying paper with the help of designers and printers. As a practical matter, you are far more likely to buy your paper through a printer than to buy it yourself and ship it to a printer. What you very much need, however, is to know your book well enough to understand what qualities the paper should have to best suit the book.

There are a few basic characteristics you will want any book paper to have. First, a book paper must be opaque enough to be printed on both sides without any appreciable amount of "show-through," which is print from one side of the sheet showing as lines or shadows on the other side, making the other side hard to read.

Second, a book paper must be white enough to provide adequate contrast with the black type laid upon it, unless the paper is purposely made of some other color than white. To use a very inexpensive, low quality, greyish or brownish paper for your book is destructively pennywise; it can destroy the entire appearance of your book and negate all your work and investment.

Third, a book paper should be capable of carrying adequately sharp and attractive reproductions of any illustrations you use. That does not mean printing a book with a few illustrations on expensive and inappropriate glossy stock. It does mean using a paper white enough and opaque enough to do decently by your illustrations—or reconsidering how and where you will use them. It is usually attractive to an author to carry illustrations in place within the book, where they will, if well-captioned, be most useful. Yet the tendency and desire to carry illustrations this way must be balanced against both the cost of paper and the risk of using the wrong paper for the text of the book, which is probably the overwhelming bulk of the book. Sometimes it is far better to run your illustrations in a single group of pages, as so many other publishers do, and for similar reasons. Then you can use two papers, one for text and one for illustrations, with both right for the images they carry.

Fourth, the book paper you use should bulk properly for the size of book you want to publish. Type sizes, page margins, and trim sizes can control the number of pages in your book; paper bulk controls its thickness. A 256-page book on excellent but rather thin paper can look no thicker than a 100-page pamphlet, diminishing its value in the eyes of a potential buyer. The same 256-page book, on bulky, slightly more porous, but still highly readable paper, may be twice as thick and be recognizable as a book of an entirely acceptable and buyable size. Commercial publishers know and act upon this kind of understanding every day; so should self-publishers.

In book papers, the question of bulk has little or nothing to do with cost or weight. A bulky paper is not necessarily more expensive or more costly than a thin one. Actually, it is very often the reverse; some of the most expensive book papers used are very thin, dense, opaque "bible" stocks, suitable for use in very large, long-lasting reference books.

How long the paper in a book will last is a matter of deep concern for most book publishers. An extraordinarily large number of the books now in libraries and bookstores will literally self-destruct in the next couple of decades because of the high sulphuric acid content of the papers used in them. That is a worldwide phenomenon; how the use of self-destructing paper in books came to be generally accepted in publishing is something for future generations to study and deplore. In this generation, though, some alternatives are now available. It is possible for any competent book production person or printer to order and use acid-free or largely acid-free paper in your book if you want your book to last. It is usually (but not always) somewhat more expensive than most equivalent self-destructing book papers, but those cost relationships are changing as publishers seek acid-free paper for more of their books. When the time comes for you to produce your book, be sure to compare the prices of acid-free and self-destructing paper so that you can make an informed decision as to which way to go. Should you have any difficulty in finding proper comparisons, calls to a few of the paper merchants and paper mills listed in *Literary Market Place* will allow you to find the information you want quickly and easily.

Pricing and Printing

It is at this stage that you bring into play the questions of pricing and printing discussed in Chapter 3, taking into account your estimated production costs, anticipated marketing costs and modes, likely revenue per book from the expected mix of sales, and the range of prices for similar books in the marketplace.

In deciding on the size of your printing, you may wish to keep in mind the rule of thumb by which many commercial houses operate: print the number of books you expect to be able to sell in the first year, and no more. Book storage often costs money, remember, and books held for long periods are subject to some of the same problems as unbound sheets held in storage. You can always print more as needed. Indeed, if pre-publication response is extremely favorable, you can even go back to press again before actual publication; be very careful of this, however, for good reviews do not always translate into hard sales, and large returns may result from large advance orders. You may sink a great deal of money into an extra printing that you will not recoup so easily.

The price itself should be set early enough to be included on your various pre-publication promotion pieces; note that, if production problems cause your costs to be much higher than expected, you can change the price on publication, if necessary. Try to avoid that, however, for it causes a great deal of confusion and extra handling in order processing. You also will want to set the price in time to be printed on the cover of the book, either on the front or back, or on the jacket. While this is not absolutely necessary, bookstores prefer that the price be printed somewhere on the book's cover or jacket for their ease of handling the book at the check-out counter. Should the price change later, the standard practice is to paste a new price over the old one with a sticker. But that again causes extra handling and some potential confusion, especially in dealing with returns, so it should be done only as absolutely necessary.

The Body of the Book

Going from composed, corrected, laid-out pages to a finished book is done in several steps, which together are the balance of the publishing process. Reviewing those steps can help identify some of the key choices to be made.

Once the pages have been completed, they are made up into *forms,* which are groups of composed pages ready to be placed upon a press and printed. For offset printing, which is the standard mode of printing used in book publishing today, the form is an offset printing plate developed photographically. The older kind of form is the metal printing plate, which is still in limited use for some kinds of periodical and special-purpose printing. For many years, the normal size of the form used in book production has been 32 pages; that is why printers and publishers often speak of book lengths in multiples of 32, such as 224, 256, 288, or 320 pages.

Forms placed on presses are then *run,* or printed, with the number of books or other publications produced called the *press run.* It takes printers time to properly place each form upon the press after removing the previous plate—often more time than it takes to print a relatively short run of that form on a fast press. That is the main reason why short runs cost so much more per unit than do longer runs.

It is quite important to know that a printer's available equipment can greatly affect the cost of a printing job. Aside from knowhow, the main reason for using an experienced short-run book printer to produce your book is that such a printer is likely to have the right equipment to do the job economically and well. Another printer, however skilled, may not have quite the right equipment. For example, a printer whose press is not quite the right size for your requirements may waste a good deal of paper. A printer with a wonderfully fast press may be superb for long press runs, but inappropriate for your book because changing plates on that press takes so long. A printer can be undertooled, overtooled, or just not quite properly tooled to competitively meet your needs. Even among experienced short-run book printers it is desirable to get competitive quotes; that is particularly so when those printers are bidding on a whole job, which involves their supply or purchase of composition, bindings, and paper. Those competitive bids must be in writing, and itemized; to have only a verbal and unitemized quote is like having no real quote at all.

Here is one example of a printer's estimate for a modest-size book of straight text:

From: Hereiam Printing Company

To: Thereuare Publishers

We are happy to quote the following specifications and 1985 prices to manufacture your title, NAME OF BOOK.

SPECIFICATIONS

Trim Size: 6″ x 9″
No. of Pages: 264 as 272 cancel 8
Quantity: 3,500 casebound
Preliminary: From your repro we will make film and plates. Plates good for one printing only. We will provide one set of blues.

Presswork: The body will print 1/c black throughout using the web offset method.

Paper: For the body you will supply basis 25x38 - 55# Heritage Antique stock, bulking 366 ppi.

Binding: We will gather printed signatures and adhesive notch bind with three piece (Kennett over multicolor sides) case material over .080 Pasted Oak Board stamped on the spine with one hit non-tarnish foil using your dies. We will case in round, loose back, affix 80# cream endsheets, trim three sides and attach one super, one line and two headbands. We will jacketwrap bound books using jackets supplied by you. Loose books will be banded on non-returnable skids and shipped f.o.b. our manufacturing plant in Hereiam, New York.

PRICES

	3,500	Add'l M's
Preparation/Plates:	$1,150.00	—
Presswork:	910.00	$ 136.58
Case Bind/Disposition:	2,581.00	473.53
Total:	$4,641.00	$610.11

Terms: Net cash thirty (30) days from date of invoice. On past due invoices, you agree to pay interest at the rate of one and one half (1½) percent per month, with interest being calculated from the invoice due date to the date payment is received.

The complexity of such a printer's estimate makes clear the advisability of getting some publishing reference books and of seeking professional assistance if your are publishing works that require any special handling. This book had no illustrations, for example, which might have resulted in much more complicated printing specifications. Note that although established publishers normally have such work done on credit, you as a self-publisher will most likely have to pay all or part of your manufacturing costs in advance, following standard business practice in dealing with unknown parties.

The author-publisher really has little hands-on work to do at the printing and binding stage, aside from looking at blueprints if necessary. At this point, you are more than anything else a buyer, and you need to be an extremely careful one, with or without the help of your own skilled production person. Turning your work from a manuscript into a printed and bound book is probably the major speculative investment you will make as a self-publisher, unless you decide to go for broke—which some literally do—in promoting your book.

Printed sheets coming off the press are *folded* and *trimmed,* sometimes as part of the operation of a sophisticated press or total production process operation, and sometimes by separate bindery machinery, which is the older production style. The resulting groups of pages are called *signatures* and keep their identity as such when sewn with their inner ends uncut into hardcovered books; that is the normal way of handling pages in such books. When trimmed on all four sides, for insertion into flat-backed, called *perfect bound,* soft-covered books, or for insertion as drilled pages into looseleaf binders, they lose their identity as signatures.

In some instances, and for reasons of economy, some proportion of the printed sheets coming off a press are not folded, trimmed, and taken on into finished books, but are held as sheets and made up into books in small groups after the initial body of books made has been sold out. Many vanity presses do that, to meet their contractual commitment to produce a certain number of "books"; they do not really expect ever to make the held sheets into books. But some publishers and self-publishers also hold sheets, in an attempt to avoid the high handling cost of putting plates back on press for a second printing.

For some quite large books this can be a reasonably good way to economize, but beware of spoilage on sheets so held in storage. Printed sheets held at a printer's, or for that mater in your own storage facility, can spoil rather easily, and you may find that many of the sheets you have been storing at some expense for several years are not really there when you want to use them. All it takes is a little mildew to spoil a whole bin-full or skid-load of printed paper. Likewise, a hot summer and inadequate ventilation can dry the paper out so much that it flakes and cracks, making it unusable. A slightly leaking outside wall, impregnation with an unwanted odor, or any of several other small disasters can befall stored paper. Given today's short-run technology, it is, on balance, probably better to go ahead and manufacture all the books you think you should for your first printing and do subsequent printings as necessary. It is now possible to go back on press, even with a longish book, for as few as 50–100 copies and still be able to sell fairly expensive books at a modest profit. Many printers advertise their short-run capability in *Small Press* and *Literary Market Place*. If you are filling library orders and bookstore reorders, for example, even a book costing you $5–$10 to remanufacture in smallish quantities can be sold profitably if its price is $19.95 or more.

Those printed sheets that are folded and trimmed are then gathered in proper sequence and made up into sets of book contents. How they are then handled depends on the desired binding. If they are to be put into a standard hardcovered book, the signatures will most likely be sewn together by the *Smythe sewing* method, which uses a continuous thread, sews all the sheets in each signature together, and joins all the signatures with thread. The sewn signatures will then be glued to a strong flexible *backing,* using any of several modern adhesives. Then—the now-sewn-and-glued contents of the book will be *cased in*—that is, pressed and glued into a *binding,* with glued *endpapers* providing the joinder between the book's contents and the inner covers of the binding. The binding will, in most instances, be made of some kind of plastic glued over binder's boards, generally called *boards,* which supply the hardness in the covers. It is also possible to do precisely the same kind of book with flexible covers, meaning essentially without boards.

If the book is to be softcovered, rather than hardcovered, and is quite slim, it can be covered in an inexpensive coated or uncoated paperback cover stock and *saddle stitched*—that is, bound together by only two or three staples, called stitches, set in vertically down the fold of cover and contents.

When the book is to be softcovered, but is thick enough to need a squared-off back, then it is *perfect bound*. This involves trimming all four sides of the folded signatures and relying upon adhesive to hold the contents of the book together and within the cover wrapped around it.

If the book is to be otherwise bound, all four sides of the signatures are trimmed. The resulting leaves of paper are then generally drilled and made ready for insertion into *comb, wire,* or *looseleaf* binders, in which metal or plastic is passed through the pages of the book, joining them together and holding them into the binder. Comb or wire binding devices are inexpensive and can make it possible to insert whole new sets of contents into the same binder periodically, as with yearly diaries. Looseleaf binders using posts or rings make it possible to insert pages in place in a book and are normally used in several kinds of topical reporting services. Rarely, a *press binder* is used, which holds undrilled pages solely by the pressure of the spring in the spine of the binder; this is an older and not very satisfactory binding method that is now little used.

How you make your book will depend upon your answers to several related marketing, cost, content, and personal inclination questions. The author who has done a small book of poetry and intends to sell it mainly as an adjunct to live poetry readings may be quite correct to create a slim softcovered pamphlet of a book, its heavy paper cover imprinted only with name of book and author, and saddle-stitched. That is by far the least expensive way to do such a book and will in no way hurt intended sales efforts.

On the other end of the spectrum, an author may intend to use a self-published book as basic outline and course material for an expensive business or financial seminar costing its participants or their corporate employers hundreds of dollars for a few days of discussion. That author is well-advised to produce the contents of the book as cut sheets, drill them for insertion into 8½"x11" or 9"x12" binder, and insert them into an expensive looking, padded, gold-stamped looseleaf binder, complete with many blank sheets for notetaking. The little book of poetry may cost 50 cents to produce in small quantity, while the ring binder may cost $10 in similarly small quantity, a difference of $9.50 per unit. That seems quite a large difference—but the poetry book may sell for $6.95, and the ring binder may contain the only substantial piece of printed material in a course costing $695, a hundred times as much.

Most self-publishing authors will be seeking less special audiences than those sought by the poet and seminar author above. Rather than relying upon personal and seminar sales, they are likely to want to move books to market at least partly through bookstores and other bookselling outlets. Conventionally hardbound or in perfect bound, flatbacked softcovers will be most appropriate, selling side by side with tens of thousands of other such books, competing hard for shelf space and bookbuying attention. Most self-publishing authors will therefore have another modest, but very significant book production cost: the jacket of the hardcover or the cover of the paperback.

Jackets and Covers

A good book jacket or paperback cover does not merely *announce;* it *sells.* Personally or by mail, you can surround your book with all kinds of effective selling talk and technique, but in a bookstore you have just a few seconds to sell a potential purchaser. That is usually so even though someone has heard of your book through publicity or word of mouth. A few people come into a store entirely ready to buy, but not many.

Many book jackets and covers do not even announce well, much less sell effectively. A jacket placed spine outward on a shelf, as most books are, had best have its title large enough to be seen from across the store or from a lower shelf; otherwise it may very well be passed over, no matter how good, needed, and wanted it might otherwise be. A title printed in very artistic black on a dark red background may or may not win design awards, but will surely be unreadable from the normal distance between an aisle browsing bookbuyer and a shelved book; it therefore might as well not be in the store for all the sales action it is likely to get.

Many books that do announce adequately still do not sell well. A title may give a potential buyer some sense of what the book is about, but subtitles and excellent selling copy on front and back covers are what it may take to draw that bookbuyer into real consideration of the book. It may be commendably modest for the self-publishing author to refrain from self-glorification on the back cover of a paperback or the inside cover flap copy of a book—but many people want to think the book they are buying has been written by someone notable.

Economize everywhere else you can but do not economize on covers if you want to sell books in bookstores and other outlets. Hire an artist who has done excellent covers for others to do one for you. You can find the right cover artist/designer in *Literary Mar-*

ket Place or through other publishing professionals you are working with.

You may also hire a copywriter to do the words on your covers, but that is not as crucial as getting the right artist. For many books, whether published by others or self-published, it is the author alone who knows enough about the work to effectively put the words on paper that will sell it. It may be very hard to find a good copywriter to do the cover copy for your book, and unnecessarily expensive, though you would be wise to have an experienced copyeditor go over your work before it is printed. On the other hand, those relatively few self-publishers who have decided to make a substantial investment in promotion may very well want to include cover copy and the securing of cover art in the arrangements they make with hired promotion and publicity people. Covers will prove extremely important in your selling efforts, especially for bookstore sales. Now then directly to the matter of taking your finished book to market.

CHAPTER 6

☆

Selling and Fulfillment

The selling process starts long before your finished book comes off the press. In the widest sense, it starts while you are writing the book, as you speak with local advertising, newspaper, and broadcast people who may help you promote it, to local booksellers who may sell it to their customers, and even to individuals who may buy the book.

In a more practical and operational sense, the selling process starts when you begin to make the pre-publication moves that will, together, provide the framework within which the book will be sold. Some of them are the pre-publication editorial steps previously discussed. The Library of Congress catalog registration and the Advanced Book Information (ABI) registration fall into this category, for example, as both bring your book to the attention of library and other bookbuyers, and make it easier to buy.

Throughout this chapter, we will be discussing selling moves, all or almost all of them costing something, either in out-of-pocket cash or in time, which for most of us is a cost. Most self-publishing authors will do some basic promoting and selling, but few will have the time or money to engage in large-scale promotion and selling. How much you do in these areas is entirely optional, beyond a few basic moves that it would be wasteful to omit. For almost every book, some sales are out there just for the informing and asking. No matter how low your selling budget or how limited your selling time, you should take at least the basic steps to inform others that your book is for sale and to make it easy for those who want it to buy it by placing it before them. At the very least, those who are geographically or professionally close to you should have a chance to buy your book. That means, at a minimum, placing your book in book outlets, at least locally and probably regionally, and placing professional books before colleagues, at least by national advertising in professional publications and probably by nationally distributed mail-order efforts directed toward that narrow market. Beyond those kinds of minimum efforts, only available time, money, and dedication impose limits. You can do a little; you can also publish a book, spend all your spare time and then all your time selling it, carry it around the country as the basis of a roadshow lecture series, and turn it—quite literally—into a career. Some have; some bestsellers and careers have been born that way, by those publishing their own books and those publishing through others.

Self-Publisher as Small Manufacturer

In a very real sense, selling is selling, whether you are selling books or furniture, whether you are self-publisher or small manufacturer, selling directly both to consumers and to the trade.

It is important to bear in mind that—with your publisher's hat on—you are usually just that: a small manufacturer, selling your books both to consumers directly and to those who resell them to consumers. Some self-publishing authors will not sell to the trade at all; an academic, for example, may sell an expensive book only through professional publications and to colleagues directly by mail. Conversely, some will sell only to the trade for resale; attempting to sell your first novel directly by mail would probably be a waste of promotion money.

There is an unusual wrinkle to bear in mind when selling books: your sales to the "trade" for resale are not really sales at all, as the overwhelming majority of "sales" by publishers to booksellers in the United States carry full return privileges. If you sell ten copies of your book to a bookstore, you may get them all back as "returns" and be obliged to issue a refund to the bookstore for the full price originally paid you.

Yet, you must still push hard to make that "sale" to the trade, for your book is competing for floor space in stores that cannot possibly hold more than a small fraction of the hundreds of thousands of books in print in the United States alone, with tens of thousands more being published every year.

For many kinds of books, you have at least regional, probably national, and possibly international audiences to reach and sell, an embarrassingly large number of possible sales moves, limited time, and usually very limited resources with which to work. You need to sharply identify those who might most logically be expected to buy your book, and spend your available time and money to reach them. That means selling hardest and most effectively to those booksellers who are most likely to be able to sell your book to its logical audiences, and selling directly, when that is warranted, to your best lists of prospective bookbuyers.

A scattershot approach to selling your book is pointless and wasteful. If your book will appeal to, at most, 1,000 specialist libraries and 4,000 professionals in your own field, by all means sell it by mail and by concentrated professional journal advertising. Use a library jobber to reach those special libraries, relying for help on the recommendations of your colleagues and reviews in specialist publications.

A broadcast press release and a strong effort to place the book in general bookstores will not help much. And if you do manage to place that kind of book in general bookstores, rather than in the few specialist bookstores that will sell it effectively, you will simply get the books back later on. In essence, they will have been stored for a little while in the bookstores, rather than in your own home, office, barn, or warehouse. On the other hand, a popular book may sell modestly in general bookstores, develop momentum, and then profitably soak up as much time as you have to put into it, itself generating the cash you need to promote it increasingly widely: all depends on the book you have created and the audiences to which it is directed.

There are several important selling things to do while your book is in production and before it is in your hands. This period is when most well-established publishers engage in the bulk of their selling activities; you may not be able to do nearly as much as they can without your book to actually show, but you can do a good deal in this period to help sell your forthcoming book.

Bound Galleys and Pre-publication Reviews

In addition to the Library of Congress, ISBN, and Advance Book Information registrations discussed earlier, one of the most useful pre-publication activities is sending advance copies of your composed manuscript to those several key publications that generally review books only before they have been published. These advance manuscript copies, usually called *bound galleys,* are uncorrected press proofs of the galleys or pages of your book, usually without illustrations and with a plain glued-on paper cover carrying only the name of book and author. Any experienced book printer will be able to supply them. They are expensive, currently running around $20–$30 each, and should be sent only to a few key review sources. It is a necessary step, though, especially for self-publishing authors, who can benefit greatly from favorable reviews in key publications and lose little from unfavorable ones. Sending pre–publication bound galleys will by no means guarantee favorable reviews—or any reviews at all, for that matter; no publication reviews more than a small fraction of all the books published in the United States each year. But you cannot get a hit unless you step up to bat; a favorable review of your self-published book can mean the sale of enough copies of your book to get your investment back, and perhaps then some.

Send pre-publication bound galleys of your book to *Publishers Weekly;* note that this periodical will very seldom review books after publication, as it is directed primarily to the book trade, which orders for resale in book outlets prior to publication. Most booksellers pay considerable attention to *Publishers Weekly* reviews, and a favorable review can mean some thousands of pre-publication stocking orders from booksellers. They will still have to sell your book, and you may get many of them back, as booksellers will be "buying" from you with full return-of-unsold-book-for-full-credit privileges—but you may get national distribution started from a single very favorable *Publishers Weekly* review.

Send bound galleys also to *Library Journal* and *Booklist,* both covering the vitally important library markets. Tens of thousands of libraries throughout North America buy directly because of favorable reviews in these publications. A "highly recommended" in *Library Journal* can mean 2,000–4,000 direct sales of your book to adult libraries of all kinds. These publications will review post-publication, but your best bet is to send bound galleys. For self-publishing authors, the importance of favorable reviews in these publications cannot be overstressed. Such reviews can mean relatively painless national distribution of your book to libraries, and the recouping of all your out-of-pocket costs—sometimes much more.

You may also find it useful to send bound galleys to the *New York Times Book Review,* for the relatively small chance that your book will be reviewed in that highly selective publication, and to *Kirkus Reviews,* though Kirkus has in some periods generated so many adverse reviews that some publishers have hesitated to send further books to be reviewed.

When you do send bound galleys, send a letter along with them, addressed by name to the publication's book review editor. Current names and addresses are carried in *Literary Market Place.* Don't be afraid to "sell" yourself and your book in your letter. Professionalism has little to do with "coolness." Tell the editor who you are, how you brought special qualifications and powerful motives to bear in writing the book, and why you are proud of the book that resulted. Be sure to include biographical material, publication date, and retail price, and, if possible, the ISBN number and Library of Congress Catalog number of your book.

Send bound galleys at least sixty days before your announced "publication date," and no more than ninety days before that date. Allowing less time than that may hurt your review chances, for books must be sent out by editors and reviews received back in time for publication. But announcing a later date may also hurt your chances; busy editors may push your book to the bottom of a more timely pile of work and forget that it's there.

Bear in mind that your announced publication date is little more than an estimate you are making as to when finished books will have moved from printer to you and then out into the hands of booksellers. It is *not* when you receive finished books, for you must take into account the four to eight weeks it will take your books to reach any booksellers who have placed pre-publication stocking orders for your book. It is safest to let your receipt of bound galleys from your printer trigger your setting of a publication date ninety days later—as long as your printer assures you that the book is going right into whatever bindery operations will be needed to produce the book. If you have any real doubt on that, hold the bound galleys until you are sure of actual production schedules and can therefore send them ninety days before your expected publication date.

Getting Usable Recommendations

Sales of your book can be enhanced by getting early recommendations from others to use on jackets and covers, and in other advertising and promotion pieces. It will not help much to have your next-door neighbor fulsomely praise your novel on the back of its jacket; but it can help your nonfiction work to carry a recommendation by a well-recognized name in its field. And it can help even more to have a well-known and respected name attached to a preface or introduction to your book, with that name under yours on jacket or cover, and on the title page.

Getting a useful preface or introduction will require previous close acquaintance to the right kind of person or a good introduction from a mutual friend. That can be a matter of reaching out to former teachers, current colleagues, or through family and friends; it will seldom be achieved cold. Someone who may write an introduction will always want to study an advance copy of your completed manuscript, long enough before it goes into production, for the introduction itself must be written and edited. Writing such a piece for a self-publishing author is a very considerable favor—even if a token payment from the author or a modest share of the author's revenues from book sales is part of the arrangement, as is often the case. It can also be rather a bother for the self-publishing author, for a slow introduction writer may badly bend anticipated production schedules and publishing arrangements, and a hypercritical one may spend a great deal of wasteful going back and forth with the author on trivial questions. Still, there can be great value in such a preface or introduction for some kinds of books—especially those appealing to narrow markets, when the author is a relative unknown. It can be very worthwhile to go after and get a preface or introduction that praises and recommends your work from someone who can influence others to buy your book.

Less important, but still quite useful, is the recommendation secured early enough to be used on jacket cover and early promotion pieces. Later, you hope to be able to join these kinds of recommendations with favorable reviews. Some such early recommendations may be available for the asking after little more than a cursory examination—if that—of a few chapters of completed manuscript or of bound galleys. A friend or colleague may very well do that for you, essentially asking you what to say. Others—and this will more often be the case—will take a much longer and harder look before publicly recommending your work; these sources should be sent bound galleys right off the press to give them time to read and recommend, if they will. Here, too, you are likely to already know or be personally introduced to those whose recommendations you solicit. But it does not hurt at all to send sets of bound galleys to a few carefully selected people whom you do not personally know, but whose recommendations you would prize, if you think their interests and yours coincide and that they might indeed favorably comment and be willing to be quoted. If you do, be sure to send a longish personal letter with the bound galleys, telling them why you admire them and their work, why you are sending them the galleys, how much their comments would be appreciated, and hoping that they would be willing to be quoted.

Early Promotion Efforts

Before your book is in hand, there are some very basic promotional preparations to be made. These involve making a list of those to whom you will be sending a press release announcing publication of your book; the writing of that press release; making a list of reviewers to whom you will be sending review copies of your finished book; the creation—but not yet placement—of any advertisements you will be running to coincide with publication; the selection of advertising media; and, if you are planning direct mail sale of your book, selecting lists, writing copy, and creating the mail package.

In these areas, you must make some very basic decisions as to the possible use of professionals, decisions that will rest considerably upon how much you are planning to spend to promote your book. If you are planning to spend $500–$1,000, and more later if the work generates the cash to do so, your promotion efforts will be very much a do-it-yourself matter. But if you have $5,000– $10,000 to spend, you may profit greatly by spending some of it on the kind of effective help you can get from those who routinely advertise in *Literary Market Place;* you are quite likely then to get far more sales for your money than a do-it-yourself effort might yield. And if you are planning to spend more than $10,000, by all means get some professional help. A single substantial ad in a national magazine may cost $15,000, and be a total waste of money for your particular book, when a few thousand spent on ads in carefully selected special-interest publications may prove enormously lucrative. A professional can advise you on the best use of your money in these areas.

The kind of book you have done will also affect this decision. If you are a professional, writing a book in your own field, with small, well-defined audiences, you may very well be able to handle promotion yourself, perhaps with the help of a competent freelance local copywriter. Then it may not matter whether you plan to spend $500 or $10,000 to promote your work, as you probably know the publications, reviewers, libraries, and selling appeals better than anyone advertising in *Literary Market Place*—and you may indeed be planning to sell your book primarily off the lecture platform. But if you are writing a general interest book, and have what seems to you a substantial amount of money to spend on promotion, by all means get professional help. It's a big country, and your promotion money can vanish tracelessly if used unskillfully. A few big non-selling ads, an expensive mail campaign that does not work— and your money is gone, when it might have been used to announce well, stir buying interest, and develop a little selling momentum to generate cash for wider selling efforts.

Press Releases and Review Copies

The press release announces your book; it should be sent to all print and broadcast media you feel might conceivably announce publication of your work. It is wise to take the time to carefully compile the list of those whom you think should receive that release, also noting which of them print or broadcast book reviews. That list should include all such media in your local area and all special-interest media that cover the particular content of your book. For example, a book about guns should be announced to all local media and all the main gun periodicals as well. A work in engineering, aimed at professionals, should routinely be announced to local media, but more more importantly should be announced to the publications of the profession. A novel or general nonfiction book should be announced locally and to a wide range of major print and broadcast media, including the wire services. *Literary Market Place* has an excellent selection of reviewing media that can be used for both press release and review purposes. The *Standard Periodical Directory,* which is found in most even modestly substantial libraries, is an excellent source for special interest publications since it breaks out its many thousands of periodical entries by interest group and supplies the kind of basic information you need for compiling your list.

The press release itself is basically a brief newspaper article. Those who announce your work after receiving your release may simply take the top of your release and print it, so be very sure to create a letterhead that includes the name of your publishing company, an address, and a telephone number. (A good example of a press release is given in Appendix 5.) Then, at the top of the release, be sure to note that your book is new, having just been published or "released," and give the name of your book and its price. In the text of the release, be sure to tell very briefly, right in the first paragraph, what the book is about, and follow that up with what you believe will make it most attractive to those you consider the book's main audiences. Also include a brief biography of yourself, the author, in no more than a short paragraph or two. For local and main professional publications, include a 5" x 7" head-and-shoulders photograph. A printed release looks neat, but a typed and double-spaced release looks more immediate and like a letter that should be read. Bear in mind that the first page of your release may be read, sometimes attentively—but that the second page may only be scanned, and subsequent pages are quite likely to be ignored by busy media people who will not take the time to boil down effusive prose into a very brief print or broadcast announcement of your book. You should be able to say whatever you have to say about your book very well in two pages or less, adapting and probably shortening your own jacket or cover copy to do so. If you find that you can't accomplish it in two pages or less, get someone who can.

Your list of potential reviewers will be somewhat shorter than your press release list, largely because many of those on your press release list do not carry book reviews. For the main national review media, *Literary Market Place* will be most helpful; for special-interest magazines, *The Standard Periodical Directory* is best. The local library will have copies of local periodicals with the names of reviewers, if any, listed. For local broadcast media, pick up the phone and ask the stations who handles book reviews; then send review copies to those people by name. You may want to call both local periodicals and local stations directly, possibly pre-publication if your book is likely to be either of general interest or to fit into special programming aimed at special interests. Then you can begin early to reach for both reviewers and potential interviewers. For example, a local-origination cable channel may very well have a cooking program on which you can effectively plug your new cookbook, or a self-help program on which you can push your new work in popular psychology.

Advertising Plans

This pre-publication period is also the best time to decide where any ads are to be placed, and to write those ads. You should not place them, however. Even though you will need lead time to meet publication and closing dates—that is, those dates after which ads will not be accepted for publication—there is time enough to place ads once books are actually in your hands. If your promised book is delayed, or is perhaps unacceptable as received from your printer, you may well be unable to pull any prematurely placed ads, wasting your precious resources.

For a general book, get some professional help to evaluate ad placements and to help write ads if you possibly can, even if that help is part-time, local, and not terribly experienced at advertising books. Even for a professional book aimed at narrow markets it may pay to get some professional help in this area. The special language of advertising alone may frustrate your efforts, even if you know exactly which ads to place where and think yourself able to write a reasonably good ad that will appeal to professional colleagues. Matters of circulation, size of ad, cost, placement, and frequency of insertion must also be considered, as well as the matter of creating an ad that sells. Most authors are entirely amateur in this area, not realizing for example that a too-small ad might better not have been placed at all.

Similarly, an ad without a coupon that allows a reader to buy the book directly may be all right for some general books readily available from bookstores, but is entirely wrong for a self-published book that may not have achieved very good bookstore distribution. Many booksellers do not much like ads that include coupons, reasoning that such ads detract from their business; they often therefore pressure commercial publishers not to sell books directly couponed by advertisements. But the self-publisher who does not include coupons, which make it easy for prospective buyers to buy, is often largely wasting the money spent for the ad.

Selection of advertising media can be an easy affair when dealing with books directed to narrow markets and a very difficult affair when dealing with general books. If there are two main magazines in your field, you may find that your scholarly or professional book is best advertised in them alone, perhaps rather prominently and repeatedly. You may also advertise in whichever library journal is best distributed in your field. But your general interest book may best be advertised to the trade in *Publishers Weekly,* to the library market in *Library Journal,* and to general readers hardly at all, as your limited promotion money may more fruitfully be spent in other ways. Certainly you may want to consider advertising in *The New York Times Book Review* if you have had a favorable review—but it hardly pays to advertise your self-published book modestly in the back pages of that review. For those rare self-publishers who can afford to advertise a financial or self-help book via full page ads in many newspapers around the country, the game is entirely different—but these are self-publishers working with hundreds of thousands of dollars in advertising budgets and with a great deal of professional help.

Robert Ringer's *Winning Through Intimidation* is a classic instance of a self-published self-help book that became a bestseller by pursuing a high-investment consumer advertising strategy. For most self-publishers, however, advertising must be more modest and selective.

Direct Mail Selling

Most self-publishing authors will properly want to do some direct mail solicitation of sales, if only to relatives, friends, co-workers, and colleagues. Do try hard to resist the natural inclination to proudly give away hundreds of copies of your work to such people. At rock bottom, their purchases of your work may make the difference between getting your cash investment back and losing much of it—and therefore between doing only one self-published book or having the cash to self-publish others. Such a mailing should include: a letter, adapted from your jacket and cover copy and press release; a coupon selling the book at full price, which also provides for multiple purchases of the book, perhaps at a small discount; and, where appropriate, a personal note from you, either separately or handwritten on the letter. This is all very much worth the effort; people close to you will buy, and sometimes in multiples, for gifts and for supply to others interested in your work—people you may not even know. You will have been talking about the book for quite some time with many people and their interest and curiosity may have been stimulated far more than you had realized. Solicit them to buy, openly and not at all shyly; they can mean a lot to you.

You may also wish to do basically the same kinds of mailings to certain kinds of lists of prime prospective purchasers, especially when your book is priced relatively high and is likely to be bought by relatively small groups of purchasers. Otherwise, the economics of mail-order selling will conspire to defeat the self-publishing author of a single book.

Some extraordinary self-publishing successes have been achieved with direct mail; Ted Nicholas' book, *How To Form Your Own Corporation Without a Lawyer For Under $50,* is one such. But mail-selling can also be an expensive trap; it must be handled well, which means first of all handling it very carefully.

Mail-selling economics are simple enough to understand; but a surprising number of self-publishers do not take the trouble to understand them and thereby either lose a good deal of money or fail to take advantage of the main selling opportunities for their books. In mail selling, you have to get at least enough cash back out of the mailing to pay for the cash you put in; that includes the cash cost of the mailing itself, of the book you supply to purchasers, and of order fulfillment and billing. If you were a full-fledged commercial enterprise, you would also have to pay for the time you put into the mailing, the time you spend fulfilling and billing orders received, and certain overhead costs. You might also then be willing to offset some costs by figuring that sales through other outlets might be enhanced by the advertising value of your mailings; but that is a very unwise supposition for self-publishers with one book to sell to make.

The same comments, in numbers, come out something like this: Assume that a mailing sent out at bulk rates comes to 25¢ per piece after you have figured in all the costs of renting an appropriate mailing list or lists, paper, envelopes, printing, postage, and professional help if any. (It may well come out higher, especially when the mailings are as small as a few thousand pieces.) That comes to $250 per thousand pieces mailed. Further assume that you sell successfully to 2 percent of those mailed, which is reasonably good for mail order efforts; that your book costs $12.95; and that total costs per book manufactured, shipped, and billed come to $3 each (a very rough and probably low approximation, but adequate for purposes of this discussion). You have sold 2 percent of 1,000 pieces mailed, or 20 books, for total revenue of $259 and have spent $250 for mailing and $60 more in cash for books sold, for cash costs of $310. Your out-of-pocket cash loss showing is therefore $51 per thousand pieces mailed, and is probably even higher, as costs here are modestly stated. You have also spent a good deal of wholly uncompensated time. If your book is a general interest book, you are highly unlikely to get even one-half of one percent per thousand pieces mailed; that is why publishers and booksellers mail by catalogue, spreading the costs involved over the sale of many books.

But if your book is a high-priced special-interest book, or a high-priced book that will be bought primarily by libraries, the numbers can change greatly. The same illustration, but with a book sold at $24.95, and allowing for the bigger book to cost $4 instead of $3 to fulfill, shows a net cash return, above costs, of $169 per thousand mail solicitations. And a big $49.95 professional book, sold by mail to a prime list of 3,000 colleagues and costing you $8 each to fulfill, can yield far higher percentage returns and profits. Even allowing only the same 2 percent return, 3,000 mailing pieces yielding a total of 60 sales at $49.95 each yields $2,997 on cash costs of $1,230 for a net after-costs cash return of $1,767. With a successful mailing like this, you can solicit the same list over and over again with the profits from the first, for a good mailing list keeps on buying, sometimes better on solicitations a few months later than on original solicitation. In this situation, a return of as little as two-thirds of one percent per thousand pieces mailed still yields an adequate net cash return over cash invested: that means you will probably be able to solicit the list many times, ultimately getting many hundreds of very profitable sales from a single, rather small, but highly responsive list, and with a very small initial cash outlay for mailings.

Should you decide to do mail solicitation on your own, do bear in mind that your coupon offer should make it possible for corporations, libraries, and other institutions to be billed by you, rather than having to attach a check or specified kind of credit card number with the order: these kinds of buyers will have to go through internal procedures to issue you a check, which will usually require a billing. But consumers—including your friends, family, and colleagues—should be required to either send a check with their orders or attach a credit card number, after you have made arrangements with a credit card company to honor such orders. Visa® is probably best for this, being most widely used and charging you less for this service than some other credit card companies. If you want to make it a little easier for consumers to buy by mail for what is essentially cash, offer a full money-back guarantee within 30 days if they are not completely satisfied with their purchase of your book. As so many mail-selling organizations have found, the rate of return for refund on this kind of offer is usually negligible.

For anything much beyond personal-contact mailings and the kind of narrow-market mailings described above, it is wise to secure professional help. Like advertising, mail marketing can be a very dangerous trap for the unwary. Many important questions surround proper list selection and use, including how to go about finding the right lists; which lists are most likely to be live and responsive; how to go about testing lists, rather than throwing money away on mass mailings that may not work; how much to pay for list rental; how to handle bulk mailings; and a good deal more. Two lists that look quite the same to the amateur may quite obviously be as different as night and day to the eye of the mail-order professional. That will also be so for the creation of the mailing package. For example, a wrong choice of too-heavy paper may cost you a great deal in additional postal costs, while an unclear offer or coupon may cost you a good many sales. If you intend to engage in any substantial direct-mail marketing activities, you will be wise to secure professional help, either from *Literary Market Place* or through local recommendations, from other self-publishers or through the recommendations of local advertising and mail promotion people.

Finding the Right Distributors

Self-publishing authors generally find it quite difficult to reach agreement with potential distributors, or to get firm orders from chains, individual bookstores, and non-bookstore outlets until there are finished books to show. A good pre-publication review in *Publishers Weekly* can go far toward curing all that, but such reviews are scarcely to be expected and planned for. If you are fortunate enough to get one, the picture changes; everything we discuss in the following pages should be moved up, with the review and press release, and perhaps advance copies of covers, taking the place of finished books to show. Normally, the period before books are in hand is a period of preparation in which you identify potential distributors and sales outlets, make some tentative approaches, and set yourself to move into action. The *American Book Trade Directory* carries substantial lists of book wholesalers and jobbers; a smaller, more selective, and therefore probably more useful list is carried in *Literary Market Place*. The latter publication also carries an essential list of most of the main book distributors and sales representatives; others, advertising in such publications as *Small Press* and *Publishers Weekly,* identify themselves as organizations wanting to represent small presses. If your book is suitable for bookstore distribution, you should explore such national distributors as *Bookpeople, Publishers West, Bookslinger,* and *The Distributors,* which together represent thousands of small publishers. Some regional and special-interest distributors may be especially appropriate for your particular book. You may, for example, reason that you will more effectively sell your book to bookstores in your own region and to chain bookstores than will any distributor representative carrying a catalog containing the books of several hundred other small publishers. At the same time, you should recognize that most booksellers prefer to deal with distributors rather than directly with very small publishers, and that where you cannot sell a store personally, a distributor may be able to sell better than your mailed flyer for your single book can. If you can get distribution by others—and for many self-publishers that is a big "if"—then a combination of personal selling and distribution arrangements is probably the best way to go. On the other hand, if your selling time is severely limited, or you are for any reason unwilling or unable to go out and actively sell your book, then you will need a distributor for your home area and someone to try to sell the chains.

You will have to sell to bookstores at 40 percent off list price, whether through others or directly yourself. Chains will demand and get 46 to 52 percent off list price, as will jobbers—not just from you, but from major commercial publishers as well. Distributors will get 12 to 15 percent beyond that, so that a distributor selling to individual bookstores will get 52 to 55 percent off list price, with you getting 45 to 48 percent of list price. For the 55 percent figure, some distributors will supply considerable promotional and fulfillment help, although some warehousing and other fulfillment help may be charged separately. The essential here is to carefully explore a potential distributor's willingness to represent you and to make the necessary economic arrangements, long before you have books in hand. If at all possible, make your arrangements early enough so that you can instruct your printer to send books to any distributors; otherwise, if they come to you, you would bear the extra cost for reshipment to distributors. Bear in mind throughout, though, that effective distribution may be hard to achieve, and that you may have to do much of it yourself, personally and by mail.

Library distribution works differently. You can sell directly to libraries, or you can use distributors, who will sell at 20 percent off list price and charge you a distributor's percentage besides. It is penny-wise to try to do it all yourself if a distributor such as

Ingram or Baker and Taylor will stock your books. Librarians routinely order from such jobbers and partly depend on information supplied by such jobbers when making buying decisions. Call library distributors early, learn what they will need to represent you best, explore if they will indeed stock your books, and use them.

Once books are in hand, preparation time is over. Then it is time to place those ads, send those review copies, send the early mailings, and go out and sell your book, personally and through orders, using all the promotional skills and techniques you can muster, and through all the outlets available.

Personal Selling

As we have seen, there are many good ways to sell your book. The surest way of all, though—and the method best calculated to earn back at least your modest cash investment—is to take your book in hand and sell it directly to others. No, it won't break you even on cash outlays, if you have put a great deal of production and promotion money into your book; then you must rely mainly on the results produced by the skills of others and the returns achieved from the media used—just as any other publisher does. And yes, it will take some of your time, and your time (as previously discussed) is a very real cost element in self-publishing, as in any other venture. But allowing for all that, there is no surer way to get at least your cash out so that you can live to self-publish another day if you wish.

Let us suppose, for example, that you have just self-published 1,000 copies of your book, and that so far you have invested $2,000 in composition, paper, print, bindery, and related out-of-pocket expenditures. You have decided to make your book a trade paperback and have set a $9.95 price.

On those books you sell directly to others at full list price you will receive $9.95 each. On those you place directly in book stores—those sold to customers rather than returned to you unsold—you will receive 60 percent of $9.95, or $5.97 each. Therefore, you can get your direct cash outlay back by selling as few as 201 books directly to others or as few as 335 through bookstores. If you sell both ways—and you should do so, if at all possible—your cash breakeven point will be somewhere between 221 and 335 sales. For book outlet sales, there may be some smallish related costs, such as for mailing, automobile expenses, or possible uncollectible bills, so you should figure that you really will break even on cash outlay somewhere between 225 and 400 sales. That is not very many sales and is well within the ability of most self-publishing authors to manage.

But breaking even is not all that is possible when you go out and personally sell your self-published book very aggressively. Astute personal selling can also make your book very, very profitable and provide greatly needed marketing money on a "bootstrap" basis as well as lunch money, dinner money, and money to live on while you are writing your next book.

Direct selling at full price can be especially lucrative, and never more so than when you are able to sell your book from a public platform. That is true whether you are a poet giving a reading from your work, a local historian detailing a Civil War battle, or a devoted quilter sharing the techniques and lore of the craft. The people in any audience you speak to have, by their presence, indicated their interest in your topic—and are a built-in, ready, and often eager market for your book. And that is particularly true of self-published books in your own professional area. If you travel the country or region to speak at professional meetings, or as a professional to lay audiences, you will be able to sell significant quantities of your self-published book month after month, year after year, far beyond cash breakeven needs and deep into profit. If you are a professional and don't yet do that kind of lecturing, then by all means let the decision to self-publish also be a decision to hit the lecture circuit. You can build your contacts and get your feet wet as a public speaker while you are writing and publishing your book, and be ready to go when your book comes off the press.

What kinds of professionals can do this successfully? Most kinds, really, unless they are unable to do so because of professional association or licensing strictures. The learning disabilities specialist who speaks to parent groups can do it; so can the psychologist, sex therapist, employment counselor, nutritionist, dietician, physical therapist, marriage counselor, lawyer, tax accountant, and financial advisor, to name just a few of the kinds of professionals who can profit handsomely by combining public speaking and self-publishing.

Professional or no, all it takes is making very sure that you have your book in hand and that you sell it from the platform and after the meeting. Before the meeting, too, if that is possible. Don't just mention it diffidently, by the way—sell it, really sell it.

Having your book in hand is a lot easier when you are self-publishing than when you are working with a commercial publisher. Most commercial publishers are simply not geared to ensure that your books will be there to meet you when you arrive at a speaking site, as literally thousands of disappointed authors have discovered over the years. No such problem with your own self-published book, though. You just ship ahead by air express, with instructions to hold for arrival, or take the books with you in your luggage. Of the two methods, and especially with relatively light paperbacks, we much prefer taking the books with you; then you need not worry about the hotel mislaying your books and can also avoid some rather expensive air express shipping charges.

Effective platform selling means mentioning your boften, reading passages from it, telling people that it is for sale at the back of the hall and what it costs, and that you will autograph any copies purchased after the meeting. People expect all that. You may do it all with a diffident and disarming grin—but by all means do it. At many all-day meetings, it is possible to set up an autographing session at a break point, perhaps before or after lunch, with press coverage arranged by the meeting's sponsors. Professional association and trade press coverage is particularly valuable here, for it paves the way for invitations to other meetings and future coverage. One of the key things to bear in mind here is that by aggressively selling your work, autographing copies, and reaching for press coverage, you are also helping to build the meeting and its sponsors. Never lose sight of the fact that authors enhance meetings and that authors who are well-known bring referred status to meetings and their sponsors. No matter how "unnatural" it may feel to push yourself and your work, do it, for it helps everyone concerned, not only you.

At some large meetings, it may be worthwhile to hire an exhibition booth from which to sell your book, whether or not you speak at the meeting. You must weigh costs carefully, though. At a national or large regional convention, such a booth may cost several hundred dollars, and if you have not spoken at the convention, renting a booth may not be cost-effective.

Traveling is not the only way to sell self-published books from the public platform. Authors self-publishing in any of the large number of subject areas covered by continuing education courses can very profitably combine teaching and self-publishing. That is, for example, how some very good cookbooks and crafts books have been born. And if you can successfully move into a combination of continuing education courses, community cable television activities, and self-publishing, you may have discovered a very profitable combination of activities, indeed. You may supply your self-published books to the sponsors of continuing education courses at a discount off cover prices; they may, in turn, supply your book as course material. That is probably the best way to handle it, but if necessary you can supply the book directly to those attending the course at cover price or a modest discount.

Selling Through Local Bookstores

Just as national review attention enhances your ability to find good distributors, sell to libraries, and do successful mail marketing, so do local and regional publicity and direct selling help your ability to make effective book outlet placements. But even without very much direct promotion and sales activity, it is possible to achieve quite good local and regional book outlet placement for your self-published book if you go out, visit the stores, and ask them to stock your book.

Many authors balk at doing that, feeling that asking bookstores to stock their books smacks too much of vulgar commercialism. Nonsense—if you've published a book, you want an audience; the odds are that you are just a little shy and need an act of will to overcome that shyness. The truth is that if you have self-published a lovely little book containing some of your poetry, for example, and want to get at least your cash out so that you can easily do another, you are going to have to sell a little. That means trying to set up some readings at which you will sell your work to those who come; it also means going to bookstores and asking them to stock your book.

As any good sales professional will tell you, selling a bookstore on the idea of stocking your own self-published book is hardly selling at all. It is the rare bookstore owner indeed who will not be willing to find a little room somewhere for a few copies of your work; people who run bookstores are seldom so doggedly commercially minded as all that. If they were, they probably would be in some other, far more lucrative line of business. And, after all, no money necessarily changes hands when a bookstore stocks your work; it is the nearest thing to a sale on consignment, except that legal matters relating to who owns the book while it is in the bookstore's hands work a little differently. If a bookstore returns your unsold book within an agreed-upon time, that return is for full credit, with the book costing the bookstore nothing but the price of shelf space for the time it stocked the book.

You will find almost all American bookstores listed in the *American Book Trade Directory*. Pick out those within as large an area as you are willing to travel to, and go to them. Not at their busiest times, though; a bookstore owner or bookbuyer in a shopping area will probably not want to talk with you about your book on a busy Saturday afternoon.

Even though no money may change hands, you still may have some convincing to do, however, for bookshelf space in a store is the subject of intense competition between publishers. What will win the day for you—and get you the placement you want—is that you are the book's author, and that the book obviously means a very great deal to you. Let that show; "coolness" doesn't place or sell books—commitment does. Beyond that, though, it is up to you to think through and then tell bookstore people why customers are likely to want to buy your books, for the bookstore owner who does not sell enough books is soon out of business.

For local bookstores—that is, those close enough to expect book purchases from your friends and neighbors—there should be no problem of placement. Most bookstores will routinely stock local authors, and many devote a shelf or two to their most recent books. That is not just a matter of courtesy to you, by the way; they can expect to sell your books to those who know you and will buy your book for that reason alone, if for no other. Indeed, some local bookstores will want autographed copies to sell, and will feature them as such; by all means supply signed copies when wanted.

Some local bookstores will be amenable to your suggestion that they advertise your book locally and organize an autographing session at the store, perhaps with some refreshments—especially if you are willing to chip in on the refreshments. Do suggest just that, and do chip in, even sharing some portion of a modest advertising cost. (That is, co-op, or cooperative advertising, in book trade jargon.) It is good publicity and can help start what may turn into a good local sale of your book. Remember that sales develop best by word of mouth, and that the way to get good sales in your home area is to get some publicity, some early sales, and then recommendations from one neighbor to another.

Bookstore people further away may take a little more convincing. They are not very likely to be convinced that your book will sell because you tell them that it is superbly written or that the subject matter is a "hot" topic. They hear that every day from publishers' salespeople, who also promise national publicity and substantial advertising expenditures. Many of them will stock your book anyway, as we have discussed, because you are coming to them as an author with book in hand, but it is wise also to be prepared to tell them about your promotion plans. If you are trying to organize readings, seminars, lectures, or classes—whatever is appropriate for your kind of book—tell them so. If you are trying for community cable TV exposure, describe your plans. If you are working on an author interview in a local or regional newspaper, say so. Make it clear that you are putting a great deal of time and attention into the promotion of your book; then their natural inclination to stock it will be reinforced enough for them to make the right decision.

Getting Wider Bookstore Distribution

It is possible to get a surprisingly wide distribution of your book through personal selling calls on individual bookstores in your local area and region. Indeed, if yours is a local or regional book, that may be your prime means of achieving bookstore distribution. You may even reach the chains as individual major bookstores; local chain managers may recommend you to home office regional buyers when home office central buying is required. And if you are to any extent traveling with your book in hand, as on a lecture circuit, personal selling calls on bookstores along the way are very much in order.

If yours is a book that calls for national distribution in bookstores, though, and you are a relative unknown—perhaps an author with a first book that you have decided to self-publish—wider distribution can become a difficult problem. As we have discussed, the overwhelming majority of booksellers do prefer to deal with established distributors and publishers, and we do recommend that you begin exploration early and try hard to find and effectively use one or more national, regional, or special-interest distributors. But that may be hard to accomplish, at least until you and your book have some early marketing successes to show. A favorable review in *Publishers Weekly* or one of the other major pre-publication review media is that kind of early success. It favorably disposes booksellers to stock your books, which is after all what distributors are concerned about.

A substantial sale to one of the major chains—Dalton and Walden are the biggest, and all are listed in the *American Book Trade Directory*—should even more surely bring distributor attention. That kind of sale is likely to be a two-step affair, the first sale being to a single chain bookstore or a regional buyer in the chain's home office and the second sale the national sale. It is only logical for the chain to want to see how the book of an unknown self-publisher is likely to do in the marketplace before making a major purchase, even though the "purchase" is only a conditional one, with full return privileges. Store space, especially in a major chain, is at a premium and is hotly pursued by all trade publishers, large and small.

It is also only logical for you to want to see how your book will do in the chains before undertaking the substantial gamble that accompanies acceptance of a major order. A chain with 7,000–8,000 stores, which wants to stock an average of eight books per store, will therefore place an order for 5,600–6,400 books. You then have to quickly—therefore probably rather expensively—manufacture those books and ship them to the chain, spending anywhere from a few thousand dollars for a smallish trade paperback to as much as $20,000–$25,000 for a substantial, rather expensive hardcover book. That is quite a gamble, considering the possibility that although the chain may sell out its first big order and clamor for more, it is at least equally probable that sales will not go well, and even very badly. You may wind up selling only a few hundred books and being swamped with thousands of returns from the chains. It happens every season to some books. Large commercial publishers lick their wounds, sell some returns elsewhere, remainder some, and offset the loss with more profitable books. But a self-publishing author with only one book can be bankrupted by a single experience like this.

Sell to chains, by all means; to single chain units, and to regional and national home office buyers. With book in hand, call the home offices of the chains after consulting the *American Book Trade Directory* and ask by name for that buyer you think most appropriate for your kind of book or geographical area. Be prepared to be referred around a bit on the phone; organizations and people change, even from the time a directory is set in type and the time you use it. When you do have the right buyer, make an appointment to see that person, if you can afford the time and money to make the trip and if he or she will see you. If not, discuss the book and arrange to send it, along with a covering letter, any favorable reviews, and any promotional material (such as your press release) that you have developed.

But it is usually far more productive to make a personal sales call with your self-published book, carrying in that kind of supportive material. Buyers cannot help but be impressed by your commitment, and although it may prove fruitless, it is far more likely to result in at least the kind of trial regional placement that is really the best way to go for both you and the chain. If you do find a chain buyer who wants to "go for broke" with your book, be careful; do your best to remember that if it all goes wrong, it is you, rather than chain or buyer, who will be broke.

You may be able to reach as many as a couple of hundred bookstores personally if you devote a good deal of time to the project over some months. You may also be able to reach thousands of substantial chain bookstores. But beyond these, there are 8,000–10,000 book outlets, spread across fifty states, that you can reach only through one or more distributors or through your own advertising and mail-order activities. If you do use a distributor, by the way, do not expect a distributor's sales representative to personally call on every bookseller to sell your book hard. Far from it;

sales representatives will be selling the work of as many as several hundred authors by catalogue in all-too-short sales calls on the larger booksellers. Many smaller booksellers will be sold exclusively by mailed catalogue. You will focus on only one book when you sell; that is one of the main reasons why you are so much more likely to be effective at personally selling your work than the most experienced sales representative in the world. The other is that the book is yours, and even the most skeptical booksellers find authors with their own works in hand hard to resist, face-to-face.

You can reach these thousands of book outlets by mail, whatever your other distribution arrangements, sending them descriptive material on your work, with an order form and with the kinds of supportive materials you would take in on a personal call—recommendations, favorable reviews, and a list of chain and other major bookstore buyers. R. R. Bowker rents bookstore lists suitable for these purposes, or test lists may be compiled right out of the *American Book Trade Directory*. Before spending $2,000–$4,000 on a major mailing to all American hardcover and trade paperback book outlets, you would be wise to test the likely response; spend a couple of hundred dollars on mail to some hundreds of bookstores to see just how worthwhile this kind of expenditure is likely to be for your book. No matter how favorable the reviews or strong the chain store placements, individual mail-solicited booksellers may still not place your book in significant quantities. Many are conditioned to working with distributors—or it may be as simple and unfortunate as their having already stocked several well publicized books on the same subject from large commercial publishers in that season. Then yours may be one too many. In mail-order work of any kind, it is essential to limit commitment and spending, until testing shows promising enough results. The occasional amateur gambler "makes it big" in mail order without adequate testing, but will always come up broke sooner or later, usually sooner.

Other Selling Opportunities

Direct personal sales, book outlet sales, and mail sales are the three main ways you can sell your book. Many books can be sold in a variety of other ways as well by reaching for definable audiences, nontraditional book outlets, and special book uses.

For example, a book on ski equipment may sell far better in ski equipment stores and ski industry catalogues than in bookstores and book catalogues. A book on French cheese may sell well in bookstores, but even better in specialty food stores. A gun book may sell best in gun stores; a fishing book in sports equipment stores. These are all what the book trade calls "nontraditional" book outlets; a striking recent development in this sort of area is the computer store, which has been able to sell large quantities of computer books to computer buyers and users.

There are also special institutional uses; a book is picked up and used as a premium, perhaps with a special cover and selling message on it. A book on personal income taxes may be used by a bank in this way; or a book on nutrition may be used as a premium by a food company anxious to show itself as public-spirited and a producer of nutritious, health-enhancing foods.

Clearly, many kinds of books do not offer such possibilities; most modern novels, works in medieval history, and satisfyingly obscure poetry are all similarly disbarred. But some books will reach their audiences and make far larger sales in these "special markets," as they are called in the book trade, than through normal distribution channels.

If you have done a special-interest book that will sell well in a particular market, you are likely to already have a very good idea where to reach for specialty outlet sales and premium sales in the field. If you do not yet know, then talk to people in the field, perhaps the very same people you contacted while doing your book. Where there are chains to sell, approach them just as you would a bookstore chain—and with the same caution. Where there are individual local stores to approach, make the same kind of personal selling approach you would with a bookstore.

Where there are companies using premiums as part of their marketing strategy, call into the home office, ask for the national marketing or sales department, and bounce about by telephone a bit until you find the right premium buyer to talk with. A caution on the premium sale, though: you may find yourself chasing a will-o-the-wisp, with repeated callbacks and meetings with committees in company headquarters in some faraway city—and with no sale at the end of it all. Premium sales, as professionals in that field know, are all too often long-drawn-out affairs, requiring expensive and time-consuming travel, repeated presentations, and protracted exposure to corporate bureaucracies. And they seldom go well by telephone and mail; personal contact is usually necessary. If you do choose to try to sell your book as a premium, do your best to locate the right buyer, do as much as you can by telephone and letter, spend as little as you can—and don't get your hopes up prematurely. A big premium sale can be worth tens of thousands and sometimes hundreds of thousands of dollars; but don't let it distract you from the main chance, which is selling your self-published book in all the ways you can, to all the buyers you can find.

After the Sale

Like any other small manufacturer, the self-publishing author must also ship and bill goods that have been sold, and store inventory. Where cash or credit card orders have been received, as from individual mail order book buyers, the obligation is only to ship. Where you are dealing with institutions and booksellers, you will have to ship, bill, and quite often rebill.

You should certainly anticipate handling the billings yourself, although shipping and warehousing can be handled either directly or through a service organization. You will need the help of your accountant in setting up proper billing procedures and will certainly need help on the matter of which taxes to charge on which sales, geographically and by kind of sale.

Most self-publishers correctly choose to handle storing and shipping themselves. You can secure the services of one of the very competent and experienced fulfillment organizations advertising in *Literary Market Place,* but that is probably unnecessary and expensive. You will have to pay something like 75¢–$1.25 per book to ship your books out of such a fulfillment organization, on top of the cost of shipping materials, and will have to pay at least a few hundred dollars per year more on top of that to warehouse your books. It may even cost a good deal more than all that; the truth is that it scarcely pays a fulfillment organization to set up a relationship with a self-publishing author doing a single book, unless that book takes off and becomes a substantial seller. And if that happens, and you do need fulfillment help, it is easy enough to secure.

You will also ship more promptly if you handle it yourself. You can receive a single order and sent it out the next day if you wish. Using someone else, you will have to send orders received on for fulfillment and wait your turn as orders are shipped; it will probably take a fulfillment organization two weeks longer to ship than it will take you to do so. For control, speed, and economy, it is far better to do it yourself; if you need help, you can turn to family and friends, or hire a local teenager to work with you part-time, for much less than it would cost to use a fulfillment organization.

For shipping, you will need a supply of heavy kraft paper envelopes of a proper size for single copies of your book if it is light and softcovered—for example, a saddlestitched little book of poetry, or even a 160-page trade paperback. For heavier single books, you will need a standard padded envelope of the right size; like the kraft envelopes, these are available from almost any substantial office supplies store. Some stores will also carry standard boxes in several sizes capable of taking larger quantities of books, as when you send multiple copies to a bookseller; these can also be secured from industrial box companies. You will also need standard shipping labels; it will probably pay to have a local printer print up some large self-adhesive labels with your return address and space for typing in at least six lines of fill-in, so that you can use them for any international shipments you need to make, as well as for domestic shipments. And you will need standard stapling and taping tools and materials; reinforced tape is advisable to keep the package securely closed.

For the actual shipping, your main choices are the U.S. Postal Service and the United Parcel Service. As we discussed in Chapter 3, shipping single copies via United Parcel costs more, but it is well worth considering, at least in the mid-1980s. At this time, United Parcel is far more reliable and much, much faster than the postal system for these kinds of parcel deliveries. Postal service is slow and erratic; a book shipment may take anywhere from a week to a month to get where it is going when the postal service handles it, while UPS consistently delivers the same book in a few days to a week. The time you save on handling complaints, the time and money you save in not having to reship "lost" orders that are just slow in arriving by mail, and the willingness of booksellers to reorder when assured of prompt shipment should more than make up for the additional out-of-pocket costs you incur by shipping via UPS. Ship books by post only if you must.

You will be able to pick up standard multi-part invoices for billing purposes and standard packing slips to include in shipments from an office supply store. The invoice is your billing, with some parts kept for your internal use and for rebilling if necessary. The packing slip will contain some, but not all, of the same information contained on the invoice. Get your accountant to help you here if you have no relevant business experience. What will take you hours of exploration—and perhaps result in expensive errors—will take any experienced accountant something like ten minutes in an office supply store. It is probably best to let your accountant pick up samples of the right invoices and packing slips from a store or some other client, bring them with you, tell you how to handle them, and work them into your bookkeeping system. You can then secure a proper supply.

Should these standard invoices need a bit of adaptation for your needs, make sure that they include spaces for the date, your own invoice number, your customer's purchase order number, shipping and billing addresses (if books are to be billed and shipped to different places), author, title, price, discount if any, net price if different from price, and any shipping charges. You may want to give a 2 percent discount for bills paid within thirty days of the date on the invoice to encourage prompt payment; that is a standard commercial practice. If you can, get a multi-part form that includes a packing slip; that slip should include all the information above, up to and including the title, and omit the pricing and billing information that follows.

You cannot expect bookstores to consistently reorder copies of your book when they come to what should be normal reorder points. Many bookstores do have excellent and reliable reorder systems, promptly reordering when stock goes down to a preset number of copies of a book. But such systems are as good as the people who work them, and even expensive computerized systems are no better than the data fed into them. It is wise to check your list of bookseller customers periodically, perhaps monthly, to see which ones have not reordered in the last few months and to call on those that are easily accessible while writing to the others and enclosing a reorder form. Selling more should also be part of post-sale activities.

Last, and a sore subject for authors, publishers, and booksellers alike, is the matter of returns. Standard practice in the book industry is to allow booksellers to return unsold new books to their publishers for full credit or for refund of cash already paid if no other current billings are due, as is the case for most self-publishers. You will not be able to fight that, even though there are those who will advise you to try. Every large publisher plays by the same rules, allowing full return privileges; you will have to do the same.

Do not pay return shipping charges, though. Some large publishers have begun to do that, but many do not—at least not yet. Aside from the cost to you, a store that has to pay to ship your book back to you may hold your book just a little longer, and sell it.

Your bookseller order form should carry your returns and discount policies as they apply to booksellers, and those policies should be firm. You might also attach or stamp your policies on your invoice. A fairly standard returns policy is one providing that books in good condition may be returned for full credit, starting ninety days after invoice date and no later than one year after that date. A fairly standard discount policy is one that provides for only 20 percent off list price for orders of 1–4 books to encourage placement of at least 5 books, and then moves to the main 40 percent discount for orders of 5–24 books. Wholesalers and chains will demand and get as much as 52 percent off list price, but you need not go over 50 percent on stated quantity discounts, perhaps allowing 44 percent off for orders of 25–99 books and 50 percent off for orders of 100 books or more.

These standard selling and fulfillment activities suffice to develop the natural audience for most self-published books. Some books have wider potential, however, and in the last chapter we explore ways to bring your books to much larger audiences if appropriate.

CHAPTER 7

☆

Making the Most of Your Self-Published Book

Once created, it is possible for your self-published book to become a very considerable asset, far beyond the rewards coming directly from self-publication. You may publish it, achieve modestly successful sales, and then move it into major sales through republication with an alert commercial publisher. You may sell the subsidiary rights that it carries with it, in its status both as book and a "property." You may use it to build valuable lists of direct-mail bookbuyers, bookseller customers, and friendly reviewers. Through your book, you can also build a considerable and very valuable reputation as an author and in some instances, therefore, as an expert.

Pickup by a Commercial Publisher

In Search of Excellence sold a decently successful 15,000 copies as a self-published book. Picked up by somebody alert to its possibilities at Harper and Row, it sold over a million copies in hardcover, becoming one of a very few all-time bestsellers. So, too, with a large and varied body of other self-published books, all the way from *Tarzan of the Apes* to *The Whole Earth Catalog.*

All it really requires is a modicum of success in the marketplace as a self-published work, followed by a strong approach to commercial publishers, as many as you—or your agent—are willing to approach. That approach can be as indiscriminate as sending a letter and copy of your book to the president or appropriate divisional publisher or chief editor of group after group of publishing companies, addressing each by name, pulled out of *Literary Market Place*. You can identify your best prospects—those companies that seem to be publishing the kind of book you have done—by studying the spring and fall announcements issues of *Publishers Weekly*, which carry the seasonal ads of most major publishers. You can also make a less indiscriminate telephone or mail approach to a number of established agents, picked up out of the reasonably good listings of agents carried in *Literary Market Place*.

You can do it more carefully and probably far more effectively if you take the time to familiarize yourself somewhat with the publishing industry and its people before publishing your book. Six months of carefully reading *Publishers Weekly* will give what you need to pick out those publishers who have recently had successes with self-publishing pickups. For example, the business book self-publisher seeking such a pickup in 1984 would have been careless indeed not to have approached Harper and Row after the success of *In Search of Excellence* or William Morrow after the success of *The One-Minute Manager*. Similarly, six months of reading the Rights and Permissions column of *Publishers Weekly* will yield the names of dozens of very active agents, probably including several who have had recent successes with just your sort of book. Either way—blind or clear-eyed—your approach may bear fruit, for by the time you make that kind of approach, you have already put substantial investment into your work and have to some extent proven it in the marketplace. It is the rare commercial publisher, indeed, who will not give serious consideration to your kind of proposal, under those circumstances.

Subsidiary Rights

As a publishing "property," your book carries with it a body of *subsidiary rights*, which you may exercise or which may be sold to others. The primary use is the form or the forms in which you publish the work; other uses are subsidiary to this use. When you publish a hardcover edition of your book, that is the primary use; paperback rights sold to a commercial publisher are a subsidiary use. But if you had published first in paperback, then your sale of hardcover rights would be a sale of a subsidiary right.

The diversity of special contacts required to make subsidiary rights sales make it desirable to have them agented, rather than trying to do them yourself—unless, of course, you have some relevant experience and think you would like to try. It may be helpful to point out that commercial publishers see "rights" as a lucrative major specialty, as do larger agencies, and employ special marketing people to handle them. Once your book is published, it should not be too difficult to get an agent to handle "rights" sales, provided that your book is the kind of work that lends itself to such sales. A book of poetry or a narrow-market professional book may not offer enough rights possibilities to get agent attention—or for that matter to engage much of your own attention in selling rights. But a hardcover that might do well in paperback, a novel that might adapt well for screen, or a work that might sell well all over the world, perhaps in many languages, all are prime rights candidates; and you should make a very serious attempt to sell those rights, preferably through agents or, if necessary, on your own. In many instances, rights sales have yielded far more revenue and the resulting works have reached far wider audiences than the original work.

Here are the main kinds of possible rights sales:

★ *Paperback rights:* Assuming that you have published first in hardcover, the right to publish in trade or mass market paper can be sold to another. This sale usually follows hardcover publication, sometimes many months and even years later, after your book has sold well in hardcover. If you do sell paperback rights, be sure to specify at least a year between original publication and paperback publication to safeguard your higher-priced hardcover sales. (That would not, of course, apply if your sale is for the purpose of replacing your self-published hardcover with a much more widely distributed commercial publisher's paperback edition, or a paperback with a hardcover.)

★ *Book club rights:* A book club may publish its own edition of your work or purchase multiple copies from you as publisher. Major clubs, like the Book-Of-The-Month Club and the Literary Guild, usually require pre-publication copies of your work, so far ahead of publication that you probably will have to send them bound galleys—but call and ask, as policies may change between our writing and your reading of this book. Sending bound galleys to such clubs is a gamble; but it may be a $40–$50 dollar gamble you are willing to make. Other smaller book clubs prefer pre-publication copies, but will often accept finished books arriving before your official publication date, and may accept books received long after. If you do not have an agent, you may have to go to book clubs on your own, at least the major ones.

★ *First serialization:* This is the right to run part (or all—but that is rare) of your work in a periodical, almost always pre-publication. It does not pay very much, but can be wonderful free advertising and third-party recommendation.

★ *Second serialization:* This is really second and any subsequent serializations, often occurring post-publication. This can pay a good deal in a major newspaper or national magazine, sometimes as much as tens of thousands of dollars, though these kinds of bonanza serialization fees are few and far between.

★ *Screen and other dramatizations:* This covers sale of your work or any part of it, such as its name, for use in movies, television, radio, stage, video-disc, or any similar forms. Fiction is most often so sold, but nonfiction has also often been sold for these purposes as well as for the development of documentary films. This, of course, is the largest bonanza rights area of all; it is the rare novelist indeed who does not secretly see his or her work as, in screen terms, another *Dodsworth, Gone With the Wind,* or *Ragtime.*

★ *Foreign and translation:* Foreign usually means English-language rights in other countries, while translation usually means sale of rights to put the work into other languages. This is something you should try doing yourself only with great trepidation. There are agents who advertise themselves as handling this kind of rights sale, though most well-established agents will handle foreign and translation rights.

★ *Condensation and adaptation:* These are seldom worth a great deal—but the right work in the hands of the right seller can result in a $20,000 or more condensation sale to Reader's Digest Condensed Books, or a smallish but potentially lucrative adaptation sale to someone wanting to convert your adult book into a children's book.

★ *Computerized database, microform, etc.:* Modern technology has spawned a grabbag of miscellaneous forms with a growing series of rights that can be sold to others, usually for very little money.

The main comment to make here is defensive: no one really yet understands where publishing and publishing forms are going in this era of very quickly developing publishing, broadcasting, and computer technology; some of these forms may be a substantial portion of the "books" of the future. If you sell rights to anyone, be very sure that these kinds of rights are not simply given away in the fine print of the contract. *The main thing to understand in selling rights is that you must be paid for any rights you convey to others, specifically by kinds of rights conveyed.* Note that if you do succeed in making any kind of rights sale on your own but have no experience in this area, you would be wise to have an experienced agent negotiate the contract for you; you can be badly hurt otherwise. Once a sale has been made, very few agents will hesitate to handle it for you, even if it is rather small, for other possibilities will then also be there for the agent. And the 10 to 15 percent you will pay the agent will be entirely worth it to you.

Self-publishers who successfully sell their books by direct mail may also be building up a substantial additional asset in the form of the mailing list they develop. A few hundred direct-mail bookbuyers will not do much for you, but a list composed of a few thousand or more bookbuyers on your specific subject may be rentable again and again if placed in the hands of a list broker and offered for rental. A list of 5,000 bookbuyers may be worth no more than $200 per rental, and perhaps only $100–$150 of that to you, once you subtract the percentage charged by the list broker and the cost of providing it to the renter. But if you do more than one book, and therefore continue to update and probably expand your list, it may come to be worth several thousands of dollars a year in rentals. This is all purely incremental income requiring no significant additional effort or expenditure on your part as you are promoting your books to that list anyway. Most direct-mail sellers rent the lists they develop, some netting large profits by doing so; so should self-publishers. You will find large list brokers specializing in books in *Literary Market Place;* by listing themselves there, they have conveniently identified themselves for you. Mailing consultants are also listed, but comparative shopping of your list among large brokers should suffice.

The lists of bookseller customers and friendly reviewers you develop have no similar direct economic uses but are valuable to the extent that you use them to distribute other books.

Building Your Reputation

An author who sells well builds a reputation, with or without a substantial body of personal promotional activities. But, as previously discussed, your book is likely to sell a lot better if you push it hard in every way you can, with great energy and without undue modesty.

The bonus you can get from promoting your book in this way is enhanced reputation, which proceeds from both increasing your audience and letting that audience see you and come to respect what you have to say. Many a lecture-circuit, traveling-seminar, or television career—usually a combination of all three—has started with a single book. A grueling book promotion tour sponsored by a commercial publisher may be helpful for quick exposure, but a more deliberate personal campaign, which increases your audience and reputation as you expand your book's audience and sales, may do more for both you and your book in the long run. By all means do it all, unless you suffer from critically disabling shyness that somehow cannot be overcome. Read your poetry; lecture to consumers and colleagues all over the country; develop a corporate seminar with your book as text and centerpiece; aggressively pursue local cable television, so hungry for programming; teach a local extension course and then move on to the local community college; become a personality, a guru, a celebrity. In America now, celebrity pays. Of course, celebrity has nothing to do with creating either art or clean expository writing—but it can help sell books, earn fees, and settle you into an authoring career as such careers are built in the United States today.

Having taken the potential self-publisher from idea through finished book, to market and beyond, we have completed the main body of this work, keenly aware that there is—as always when briefly discussing a whole profession and set of industries—much more that can be said. We hope this book has effectively introduced all the main matters connected with self-publishing and that it incorporates enough of the main sources of help in the field to make it possible for an author to understand the right questions, avoid the main pitfalls, and go ahead to self-publish a book.

Now follow a discussion and listing of some main reference tools and sources, and a glossary of some of the main terms encountered in self-publishing. The index will give more specific references to discussion of various terms in the text. Also included here is a list of standard proofreading and editing marks, with examples of how they are used in editing manuscript, marking manuscript for composition, and making corrections or changes on proof.

APPENDIX 1

☆

Sources of Information

Individuals planning to publish their own work will find many large bodies of published information to draw upon. All kinds of people offering professional help, tens of thousands of booksellers and librarians, and millions of names on mailing lists are all easily reachable through the pages of the many standard information sources available. Scores of books covering in aggregate every aspect of publishing also exist, including at least two score devoted to self-publishing. The wealth of material available to those in the publishing industry stems from the nature of the industry itself, which is full of people who quite normally and predictably tend to write and publish about what they know best—their own industry. Indeed, no other industry as small as publishing has generated nearly the body of information sources. And it *is* a small industry, by the way; for all its supposed glamour many individual American corporations are far larger than the entire publishing industry, even including the periodical portion of the industry.

Insight is always much harder to achieve than information, however. A beginning self-publisher may wade through many publications of all kinds, speak to many of the wrong people, and never find the right sources to develop insight and information.

You will start best by seeking other self-publishers, people who have gone through it all before you, and who have—perhaps rather painfully—learned how to ask the right questions about self-publishing and to avoid the worst pitfalls along the way. You are likely to find other self-publishers—and for that matter most small publishers, whether they publish their own work or the work of others—very willing to talk to you. Most will tell you about their experiences; recommend (or warn you away from) freelancers, printers, and suppliers of all kinds; discuss marketing techniques; and in short treat you as a new member of their "club." For most, that is exactly what it is—a national and international fraternity of small publishers, drawn together by a shared love of writing and books and thinking of itself very much as a "movement." Many will speak of it as the small press movement and quite consciously welcome you into it.

You will be able to find some of them locally through a bookseller who acts as informal clearinghouse and carries many local small-press books. You will find others through local special-interest circles, and simply by word of mouth, once you begin to ask around. You will find others—thousands of others, some of whom will turn out to be local and unknown to you—through some standard sources that follow here. Some of those you most want to listen to will be writing in or interviewed in some of the periodicals listed.

But small press movement or not, publishing is publishing. If you want to learn enough to publish and market your book well and cost-effectively, you had best learn to use the tools of the trade. You will profit greatly every step of the way—especially if you want to take your self-published book out into the wider worlds of commercial and international publishing—by using such publisher's tools as *Literary Market Place* and *Publishers Weekly* and the others we list and discuss below.

Please note that we have included prices as of this writing but that by the time you read this book those prices may have gone up, perhaps more than once. Where we think you might be well advised to buy something expensive, we say so and tell you why. Most of the large reference books and periodicals discussed first are to be found in local libraries, and certainly in large regional libraries, as they are extensively used by the public and as librarian's tools. The smaller works that follow are, as of this writing, all in print and can be purchased, though some are not found in very many libraries.

Here then are a group of published sources—selected from the otherwise possibly bewildering body of works available—that we consider very useful for people who want to publish their own works.

Literary Market Place (LMP), published annually by R. R. Bowker Co., 205 East 42nd Street, New York, New York 10017, at $45. If you buy nothing else in the way of publishing trade tools, buy this book. It is far and away the best source of practical publishing help available. If it did not exist, the book you are now reading would have to be at least twice as long to attempt to list even a smallish fraction of the basic material covered.

Literary Market Place provides all kinds of key services and suppliers, including:

——*Printers and manufacturers,* many of whom advertise themselves as handling short runs and providing complete post-editorial services. It also supplies paper merchants and mills, but you are unlikely to order your paper directly.

——*Editorial services* of all kinds, from those doing single functions to those offering to take your book all the way from idea to finished manuscript. Many of these are also quite ready to shepherd your book all the way through the production process to finished books as well. *LMP* also indexes editorial services by kind of service offered.

——*Artists and art services,* also indexed by kind of service offered; many of these offer complete book design and layout services.

——*Direct mail services* of all kinds, also indexed, and including brokers, printers, mailers, and mailing package creators.

——And many more kinds of services and suppliers, including *book exhibitors* at meetings and conventions, *photographers, shippers, translators, word processors, bookbinders, consultants, public relations services,* and *advertising agencies,* among others.

The great virtue of *Literary Market Place* in regard to suppliers of all kinds is that the listings are self-selecting. Every person or organization listed here wants to do business with publishers and holds itself out as experienced in doing that kind of business. If you comparison shop a book manufacturing or mailing job out of *LMP,* you are quite likely to find somebody who will do your work well and competitively; if you do so in your local area, you may find no one proper to work with, and probably won't even know it, being inexperienced yourself. If you seek editorial help out of *LMP,* rather than out of the local community college English department, you are likely to find competent, and sometimes superb help. The same is true for every category; this is the prime source for American book publishing.

LMP also contains substantial lists of *literary agents,* including most full-time and active American agents.

It is also a prime source from which you can compile a *reviewer's list,* as it carries substantial lists of key book reviewers in all print and broadcast media. In practical terms, you will usually need only add local and special interest publication reviewers to make up your reviewer's list.

LMP also carries a list of many *book clubs,* to which you will want to try to sell subsidiary rights to your book.

There is more: *LMP* carries a very substantial list of national and regional *distributors,* so important to many self-publishers, and an even longer list of *wholesalers.*

It also carries a list of the country's main *remainder wholesalers,* should you ultimately need to dispose of overstock.

It also carries listings of a wide selection of periodicals and reference works, covering every aspect of publishing and its related fields.

At the back of the book, *LMP* includes a Yellow Pages section, carrying the names, addresses, and telephone numbers of thousands of people listed under their organizations in the book.

Publishers Weekly, published weekly by Bowker at $59 per year. This is the single most important publishing industry periodical published in the United States; if you want to give yourself a short course in practical publishing as part of the self-publishing process—and you should want to do so—then immerse yourself in *Publishers Weekly* during the course of a year's subscription. Every aspect of publishing, large and small, is covered in the course of any year, with special issues devoted to spring and fall book announcements and special issues throughout the year devoted to several kinds of special-interest publishing and to particular markets. If you cannot see your way clear to spending the $59, then go to the library every week and spend at least an hour reading the publication from cover to cover. It is far better to subscribe, though; then you can relate articles, clip and copy, and build up a file relating to your publishing needs and interests. You can also then go back and reread; what seemed unimportant at one point may seem vital a little later on as you move through the publishing process. Almost every library of moderate size will have a subscription, though you may have to ask for it and pry it away from librarians for your own reading; it is a prime librarian's tool as well as a prime publisher's tool.

Whether you read at home or in the library, make sure that you follow several kinds of continuing matters, as well as the content of special issues and of leading articles of interest.

——Follow the "News of the Week" and the "Trade News" sections; although much will seem irrelevant for you, together they will tell much about what is being published in your area of interest, what is doing well and why, and what you can expect when you move out into the marketplace to do business.

——Follow the "Book Design and Manufacturing" section, which often covers matters of interest to small publishers, as when it covers printers using new production processes that make short runs cheaper and therefore more attractive than ever before.

——Follow the advertisements—all of them. Together, they will tell you how publishers are going about selling books to booksellers, with what offers and in what formats, which suppliers are stressing their small press capabilities, what new mailing lists and valuable sources of information are available, and a great deal more.

——Follow the "Rights and Permissions" column, which will tell you a great deal about which books are being sold to whom and by whom for all kinds of subsidiary rights purposes. A close reading of this column for even several months will identify many active agents, some general and some specialist, who can be called upon to handle your book when the time comes to move it beyond its basic self-publishing form into other print and broadcast forms, and abroad.

Publishers Weekly gives you all of this, and a good deal more, including new legal pitfalls as they develop, bestsellers, and a large body of book reviews. In short, every publisher—and especially a neophyte publisher, who will get the most from it—should read it with great care.

The COSMEP Newsletter, published monthly by The International Association of Independent Publishers, P.O. Box 703, San Francisco, California 94101. This newsletter provides a great deal of current material useful to self-publishers. Yearly membership is $40; if you prefer not to join, but want the newsletter, it is still $40. As this newsletter may not be readily available at libraries in your area, do subscribe for a year if you feel you can afford to do so. You are likely to learn a lot you need to know—and save a good deal more than the $40 you spend—by subscribing. You may also find it is valuable, depending upon the kind of book you are doing, to rent certain small-press-oriented mailing lists through the association, and to exhibit your book through the association.

Small Press, published bi-monthly by Bowker at $18 per year. This magazine is aimed directly at small press publishers, including self-publishers. As of this writing, it is relatively new, having commenced publication with the September-October 1983 issue. We found its first few issues useful, but whether or not you want to spend the money to subscribe should rest upon your examination of some back issues in a local library.

The International Directory of Little Magazines and Small Presses, published annually or bi-annually by Dustbooks, P.O. Box 100, Paradise, California, at $17.95 in paper and $29.95 in hardcover. This prime source will help you to locate small press publishers in your own area, including those sharing your kind of publishing interests; it carries subject and regional indexes.

Bookmaking: The Illustrated Guide to Design/Production/Editing, by Marshall Lee, published in 1979 by Bowker at $32.50. We highly recommend this excellent work, which covers every significant aspect of design, production, and editing. It is intended for beginning and working professionals in these fields, but is written so clearly that any beginning self-publisher, with no experience in these areas, will profit greatly from reading and using it. It also contains an excellent bibliography.

American Book Trade Directory, published annually by Bowker at $89.95. This is the most complete and up-to-date directory available, covering 20,000 American and Canadian bookstores, 7,000 distributors and wholesalers, and other bookselling organizations and people, and carrying such vital information as kinds of books and buyers by name. It serves as the basis for Bowker's bookstore and wholesaler mailing lists, which may be rented, should you wish to make direct selling mailings to bookstores and wholesalers. You should find this directory available in many moderate-sized and all large regional libraries.

Note that you need not rent the Bowker lists, especially if you want to do small local or regional mailings, or to compile a small, complete prospect list of bookstores and wholesalers you want to call on personally. Then you can work directly from a library copy of the directory.

American Library Directory, published annually by Bowker at $89.95. This is an up-to-date directory of over 35,000 American and Canadian libraries of all kinds, broken down in several ways, including size of bookbuying budget and kinds of materials purchased. It serves as the basis for Bowker's library mailing lists, which (like the bookstore and wholesaler lists derived from the book trade directory) may be rented. You may want to do some targeted special mailings out of the book or the rented lists, even while relying upon specialist library jobbers for the main library sales of your book. It is available in most libraries as it is a prime librarian's tool.

Direct Mail List Rates and Data, published quarterly by Standard Rate and Data Service, Inc., 5201 Old Orchard Road, Skokie, Illinois 60077, at $92 per year. This is the standard list selection and ordering tool used by mail order professionals. It identifies, describes, and provides full ordering information on approximately 50,000 business, consumer, farm, and cooperative mailing lists. Should you decide to go on your own into considerable special interest or general mailings to sell your book, this will be the basic tool you will need. You will not find it available at most libraries, however, although some large regional libraries will have it. Although modest personal, local, and special interest mailings from your own smallish compiled lists can easily be handled personally, we urge you to use professionals for anything more ambitious. Mail selling is very much a specialist's game; amateurs beware.

Ayer Directory of Publications, published annually by Ayer Press, 1 Bala Ave., Bala Cynwyd, Pennsylvania 19004, at $66.

Standard Periodical Directory, published every few years by Oxbridge, Inc., 40 East 34th Street, New York, New York 10016, at $120.

Both of the above are standard advertising industry tools available in most libraries; between them they will supply the basic information you need to place advertising, should you decide to go into such publications as special-interest magazines on your own. Note that we feel it much better to do such placements through an agency or freelancer who "knows the ropes"; doing so can save the inexperienced some costly errors.

Audiovisual Market Place, published annually by Bowker at $39.95. This is the audiovisual industry equivalent of *Literary Market Place* and is found in most libraries. You will find it quite useful if you want to include an audiovisual component in your work, as when an audio record is inserted in a book cover pocket.

International Literary Market Place, published annually by Bowker at $55. This is an international publishing equivalent of *Literary Market Place* and will be useful should you decide to try to handle the sale of international rights or set up international distribution arrangements on your own, as it carries the key people and organizations you will then want to reach.

How To Publish Your Own Book, by L. W. Mueller, published in 1978 by Harlo Press, 50 Victor Avenue, Detroit, Michigan 48203, at $5.95. This is a fine basic book for self-publishers, and we urge you to buy and carefully read it (side by side with ours, we hope). Lothar W. Mueller runs the Harlo Printing Company, which has for many years done a considerable volume of self-published books, and his book reflects a great deal of hands-on experience in every aspect of manuscript handling and book production. He should certainly be one of the skilled people you plan to call upon quite early in the self-publishing process.

The Publish-It-Yourself Handbook, edited by Bill Henderson, published in 1980 by The Pushcart Press and Harper and Row, 10 East 53rd Street, New York, New York 10022, at $6.95. This is a very good collection of self-publishing experiences, plus a modest selection of how-to observations on the self-publishing process; it is well worth reading.

The Self Publishing Manual, by Dan Poynter, published in 1980 by Parachuting Publications, P.O. Box 4232, Santa Barbara, California 93103, at $9.95. This book on the whole process of self-publishing carries many useful observations and will be particularly useful for those publishing to special interests and focusing on special (rather than normal booktrade) channels to take their books to market.

How To Self-Publish Your Own Book and Make It a Best Seller, by Ted Nicholas, published in 1980 by Enterprise Publishing, Inc., 725 Market Street, Wilmington, Delaware 19801, at $4.95. This book on self-publishing covers a wide range of small business, publishing, and related matters. It will be most useful to those who decide to do all or almost all of the functions involved themselves, with little other professional help, and is strongest in its treatment of mail order and advertising matters.

How To Get Happily Published, by Judith Appelbaum and Nancy Evans, published in 1982 by New American Library, 1633 Broadway, New York, New York 10019, at $6.95. This book for writers deals mainly with how to find and successfully work with a commercial publisher, but includes a useful section on self-publishing.

How To Start, Run, and Stay In Business, by Gregory F. Kishel and Patricia Gunter Kishel, published in 1981 by John Wiley & Sons, 605 Third Avenue, New York, New York 10158, at $7.95.

How To Run a Small Business, by the J. K. Lasser Tax Institute, published in 1982 by McGraw-Hill Book Company, 1221 Avenue of the Americas, New York, New York 10020, at $17.95.

There are scores of sound books on how to start and run a small business—which is what you are doing when you publish your own book. The two books above each cover the main necessary matters competently, and are clearly written.

Among the various professional associations, you may want to consider joining the Author's Guild, especially if you have published at least one book already. Although much of the Guild's attention is focused on the relationships between authors and commercial publishing houses, they provide much useful information and guidance on questions of copyright, libel, invasion of privacy, and the like, both in the initial packet of materials sent to new members and in the quarterly *Author's Guild Bulletin.*

APPENDIX 2

☆

The Self-Publishing Process

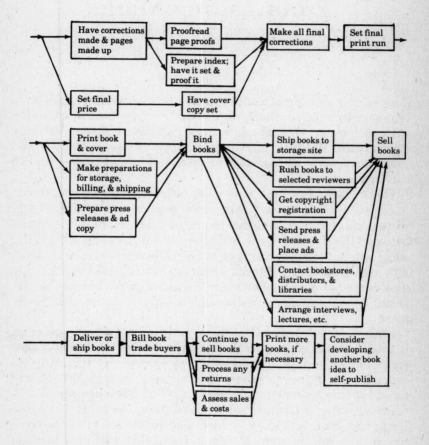

APPENDIX 3

☆

Copyediting and Proofreading Marks

Copyediting and proofreading marks form a special small sublanguage by which authors, editors, and compositors communicate with each other. Over the centuries they have become relatively standardized, so that even strangers, working together for the first time, can specify with assurance details of format so essential to each work.

These marks are used somewhat differently at various stages in the publishing process. During the writing and developmental editing stage, copyediting marks are generally made in the spaces between the lines or in the wide margins of the page. This is the stage where the manuscript receives its heaviest editing. Indeed, although some inexperienced writers expect to produce clean copy first crack out of the typewriter, the manuscripts of most professional writers at this stage resemble nothing so much as battle maps.

Once the developmental editing is finished and a final typescript is produced, the copyeditor does a much lighter editing of manuscript. At this stage, the aims are to correct any lingering inconsistencies in the manuscript and to specify necessary details of format to compositors, a process often called typemarking.

Proofreading is handled somewhat differently. After the manuscript has been composed, galleys and proofs are read for typographical errors or errors of format. Inevitably, too, other kinds of errors emerge on this proofreading, for the manuscript always looks different—no matter how experienced the eye—when it is set in type. But this is no longer double-spaced manuscript with room for changes between the lines. For clarity and accuracy, all changes and corrections at the proofreading stage are made in the margins to the left or right of each line; if multiple changes are to be made on a line, they are separated in the margins by diagonal lines (virgules). Only marks indicating where changes are to be made appear in the body of the text, and are always flagged in the margin, to be sure they are not overlooked by the compositor as the corrections are being made. Authors—and especially author-publishers—should carefully mark their changes either PE (Printer's Error) or AA (Author's Alteration), since the charges for these may be in dispute if the amount of changes is large.

Following is a table of the main copyediting and proofreading marks in use today, and then a brief example of how these marks are used in marking the same piece of copy at the three main stages mentioned above.

Copyediting and Proofreading Marks

Mark	Instruction
ℓ	Delete marked copy
⊂ or ( )	Close up space
ℰ̃	Delete marked copy and close up space
stet	Restore indicated matter, formerly marked for deletion
∿	Transpose letters or words indicated
∧	Insert matter to copy where indicated
¶	Start new paragraph
No¶ or ⌐	Run on, without starting new paragraph
☐	Indent copy by number of ems indicated
⊡	Indent whole section of copy (hang indent)
◨	Indent copy by one en
[	Move copy to the left
]	Move copy to the right
] [	Center copy in column or image area
⊓	Move copy higher

⊔   Move copy lower

=   Align type horizontally

‖   Align type vertically

Insert space

Eq#   Equalize spacing

Sp   Spell out

———   Set underlined copy in italic type

∿∿∿   Set underlined copy in boldface type

≈≈≈   Set underlined copy in boldface italic type

rom   Reset indicated copy in roman type

Ital   Reset indicated copy in italic type

bf   Reset indicated copy in boldface type

bfital   Reset indicated copy in boldface italic type

≡   Set in large capital letters

=   Set in small capital letters

==   Set first letter in large capitals, rest in small

/   Change capital letter to lower case
(Also used to separate changes in copy margins or text)

?   Doublecheck matter

⊙   Insert period

∧   Insert comma

∨   Insert apostrophe

❨ ❩   Insert quotation marks

∨   Insert superscript

∧   Insert subscript

∧   Insert semicolon

⊙   Insert colon

=or-C   Insert hyphen

m̄   Insert an em dash

n̄   Insert an en dash

or ld   Insert space (leading) between lines

lig   Use ligature where indicated

↶   Move encircled copy to indicated spot

(out...see copy) Pick up copy omitted in composition

Do not set encircled comments to editor or compositor

hr# Leave hair space between letters

.... or... Insert ellipses where material was cut from quotation

Copyediting and Proofreading Marks

Manuscript in Development

Chapter ~~Ten~~ 10

T~~HE~~ INCENSE RO~~A~~D

¶ And when the queen of Sheba heard of the fame

of Solomon... ⌐

¶ ⌐she came to Jerusalem with a very great train,

with camels that bare spices, and very much gold, and

precious stones...

~~10 And she gave the king an hundred and twenty talents...~~

I: 1-10

(¶ Kings)

On her way to the l~~b~~nd of Israel, the Queen of Sheba

carried

followed the old Incense Road, which ~~brought~~ spices and

north from Arabia ⊙ ---one of early

other goods ~~desired for religious use~~ to the great kingdoms

along the Mediterranean Sea, --

stet   For over 1500 miles the ~~caravan~~ trail wound through ~~rocky~~

rock-bound

~~desert~~   gorges from the Hadramaht to Jordan and Syria.

∧

Manuscript in Copyediting and Typemarking:

Chapter 10

The Incense Road

And when the queen of Sheba heard of the fame of Solomon...she came to Jerusalem with a very great train, with camels that bare spices, and very much gold, and precious stones...

(Kings I: 1/10)

On her way to the land of Israel—one of the many great early kingdoms along the Mediterranean Sea—the Queen of Sheba followed the old Incense Road, which carried spices and other goods north from Arabia.

For over 1500 miles the caravan trail wound through rock-bound gorges from the Hadramaut to Jordan and Syria.

Galleys for Correction:

CHAPTER TEN

THE INCENSE ROAD

And when the queen of Sheba heard of the fame of Solomon . . . she came to Jerusalem with a very great train, with camels that bare spices, and very much gold, and precious stones

(I Kings: 1-2)

On her way to the land of Israel—one of the many great early kingdoms along the Mediterranean Sea—the Queen of Sheba followed the old Incense Road, which carried spices and other goods north from Arabia.

For over 1500 miles the caravan trail wound through rockbound gorges from the Hadramaut to Jordan and Syria.

APPENDIX 4

———————————— ☆ ————————————

Type Specimen Sheet

TIMES ROMAN

ABCDEFGHIJKLMNOPQRSTUVWXYZ
abcdefghijklmnopqrstuvwxyz $1234567890

When choosing a type for your book, you will look at type specimen sheets, like this one, showing the basic font of the type and a sample of text in print. Before making a final choice, have at least one full page set in your desired type, so you can be sure it is readable in large blocks.

HELVETICA

ABCDEFGHIJKLMNOPQRSTUVWXYZ
abcdefghijklmnopqrstuvwxyz $1234567890

When choosing a type for your book, you will look at type specimen sheets, like this one, showing the basic font of the type and a sample of text in print. Before making a final choice, have at least one full page set in your desired type, so you can be sure it is readable in large blocks.

OPTIMA

ABCDEFGHIJKLMNOPQRSTUVWXYZ
abcdefghijklmnopqrstuvwxyz $1234567890

When choosing a type for your book, you will look at type specimen sheets, like this one, showing the basic font of the type and a sample of text in print. Before making a final choice, have at least one full page set in your desired type, so you can be sure it is readable in large blocks.

KORINNA

ABCDEFGHIJKLMNOPQRSTUVWXYZ
abcdefghijklmnopqrstuvwxyz $1234567890

When choosing a type for your book, you will look at type specimen sheets, like this one, showing the basic font of the type and a sample of text in print. Before making a final choice, have at least one full page set in your desired type, so you can be sure it is readable in large blocks.

BODONI

ABCDEFGHIJKLMNOPQRSTUVWXYZ
abcdefghijklmnopqrstuvwxyz $1234567890

When choosing a type for your book, you will look at type specimen sheets, like this one, showing the basic font of the type and a sample of text in print. Before making a final choice, have at least one full page set in your desired type, so you can be sure it is readable in large blocks.

JANSON

ABCDEFGHIJKLMNOPQRSTUVWXYZ
abcdefghijklmnopqrstuvwxyz $1234567890

When choosing a type for your book, you will look at type specimen
sheets, like this one, showing the basic font of the type and a sample of
text in print. Before making a final choice, have at least one full page set
in your desired type, so you can be sure it is readable in large blocks.

JANSON ITALIC

ABCDEFGHIJKLMNOPQRSTUVWXYZ
abcdefghijklmnopqrstuvwxyz $1234567890

---

*When choosing a type for your book, you will look at type specimen sheets, like
this one, showing the basic font of the type and a sample of text in print. Before
making a final choice, have at least one full page set in your desired type, so you
can be sure it is readable in large blocks.*

MELIOR

ABCDEFGHIJKLMNOPQRSTUVWXYZ
abcdefghijklmnopqrstuvwxyz $1234567890

When choosing a type for your book, you will look at type specimen sheets, like this one, showing the basic font of the type and a
sample of text in print. Before making a final choice, have at least
one full page set in your desired type, so you can be sure it is readable in large blocks.

GARAMOND

ABCDEFGHIJKLMNOPQRSTUVWXYZ
abcdefghijklmnopqrstuvwxyz $1234567890

When choosing a type for your book, you will look at type specimen sheets, like this one, showing the basic font of the type and a sample of text in print. Before making a final choice, have at least one full page set in your desired type, so you can be sure it is readable in large blocks.

ELECTRA

ABCDEFGHIJKLMNOPQRSTUVWXYZ
abcdefghijklmnopqrstuvwxyz $1234567890

When choosing a type for your book, you will look at type specimen sheets, like this one, showing the basic font of the type and a sample of text in print. Before making a final choice, have at least one full page set in your desired type, so you can be sure it is readable in large blocks.

APPENDIX 5

☆

Sample Press Release

NEWS FROM WILEY

FOR IMMEDIATE RELEASE   CONTACT: Cynthia Kirk
212-850-6497

CAREER COMPANION SERIES LAUNCHED

WITH MANUALS FOR MANAGERS AND SALESPEOPLE

Advance praise for THE MANAGER'S ADVISOR:

"Contains much valuable, practical advice...its most attractive
feature is the authors' assertive, persuasive and enlightening
narrative voice...Sound counsel for the new breed of 'cool'
supervisors."--ALA Booklist

and for THE SALES PROFESSIONAL'S ADVISOR:

"The advice is serious, professional, empathetic and soundly
reasoned. Recommended for professionals both on the road and at
home."   --Library Journal

    David Brownstone and Irene Franck's THE MANAGER'S ADVISOR

($39.95) and THE SALES PROFESSIONALS ADVISOR ($34.95), recently

published by Wiley, are not typical management or sales

handbooks. While techniques are covered, the emphasis throughout

is on the progress of a career, not on the mechanics of doing

the job. Believing that these are difficult times for every

professional, the authors have designed a special series of

personal career companions.

    According to the authors, it's a pipe dream to assume that

companies will be ever profitable and consistently able to

reward employees with high pay during the working years and

substantial pensions at retirement. Therefore, the authors

maintain that long-range financial and professional development

planning is essential. THE MANAGER'S ADVISOR and THE SALES

PROFESSIONAL'S ADVISOR lay the groundwork for the kind of

-more-

JOHN WILEY & SONS, Inc. · 605 Third Avenue, New York, N.Y. 10158 · (212) 850-6000
New York · Chichester · Brisbane · Toronto · Singapore

CAREER COMPANIONS, Page 2

personal planning which will allow the individual to adapt to rapid changes in the work environment.

At the heart of both books, then, are practical and personal concerns, such as:

* getting started, moving up, effective job changing and alternative careers;

* time management and effective communication skills;

* compensation and financial planning, appearance, and job-related problems such as stress, alcoholism, and loneliness.

However, each also addresses the specific concerns of its readership.

THE MANAGER'S ADVISOR deals with understanding computers and the new tools of the automated office; organizing and conducting successful meetings; selecting, training and holding key employees; maneuvering through company politics; and controlling the flood of paper, telephone calls and meetings which threatens to inundate every manager.

THE SALES PROFESSIONAL'S ADVISOR focuses on prospecting leads; efficient use of the telephone; appointment-getting techniques; mastering the selling process from stating the benefit to overcoming objections to closing the sale; and handling reports, forecasts and travel & entertainment expenses. Each book includes several personal case histories to illustrate problems specific to the profession, a glossary and an annotated list of sources for information which has been cited as "excellent" by ALA Booklist.

-more-

CAREER COMPANIONS, Page 3

    Brownstone and Franck urge choice and control on their
readers. Their cogent, practical advice is a guide to moving
ahead in these uncertain times.

    DAVID M. BROWNSTONE spent many years in sales and management
before turning to a very active writing career. He is general
editor of and a contributor to Wiley's Small Business Series. He
has written several other books for Wiley, including SELL YOUR
WAY TO SUCCESS, the award-winning, WHERE TO FIND BUSINESS
INFORMATION (with Gorton Carruth), now in its Second Edition,
and PERSONAL FINANCIAL SURVIVAL (with Jacques Sartisky).
    IRENE M. FRANCK was a manager and management trainer before
becoming a writer and editor. She was editor of Wiley
Self-Teaching Guides for ten years and developed more than 80
books in that series.
    DAVID BROWNSTONE and IRENE FRANCK are husband and wife,
fellow members of The Hudson Group and co-authors of The VNR
Dictionary of Business and Finance and The VNR Investor's
Dictionary. They live in Chappaqua, New York.

THE MANAGER'S ADVISOR
David M. Brownstone and Irene M. Franck
0-471-86346-7;   584 pages; $39.95
Publication Date: October, 1983

THE SALES PROFESSIONAL'S ADVISOR
David M. Brownstone and Irene M. Franck
0-471-86352-1;   562 pages; $34.95
Publication Date: December, 1983

We always appreciate tearsheets of your reviews of Wiley books.
                       ######

To request a review copy of

____ BROWNSTONE: MANAGER'S, 1-86346-7

____ BROWNSTONE: SALES, 1-86352-1

please send your NAME_____

                PUBLICATION_____

                ADDRESS_____

                         _____

to: Ms. Cynthia Kirk
    John Wiley & Sons
    605 Third Avenue
    New York, NY 10158

    212-850-6497.

---------------- ☆ ----------------

Glossary

In any new field, learning the language is often half the battle. And the language of publishing can be rather daunting to self-publishing authors, who often feel as if they were drowning in a sea of unfamiliar terms, especially when dealing with production and editorial people. Here then is a relatively brief selection of such commonly encountered special terms, arranged and related for easy understanding. Where a term has been discussed in the main text of this book in more detail, or is better set in context there, we say so, referring you to the chapter in which it is discussed.

You may also want to purchase either Brownstone and Franck's *Dictionary of Publishing* (Van Nostrand Reinhold, 1982) or Jean Peters's *Bookman's Glossary* (Bowker, 1983).

addenda, errata, corrigenda: The book world still uses quite a substantial number of words like these, left over from the Latin and Greek that were for so long the main languages of educated Europeans. In some instances, they are not even leftovers, but instead pretentious pseudo-Latin terms. These three are merely jargon, with clear modern English equivalents; you need to know what they mean, rather than use them in your book, for they are sometimes confusingly used as synonyms. *Addenda* are brief additions to an already printed book, pasted or otherwise fixed onto an already bound book or bound into a printed but as yet unbound book. *Errata* are errors, likewise affixed or bound in. *Corrigenda* is a synonym for errata.

author's alterations (AAs), printer's errors (PEs): These terms raise

the ever-vexing question of who did what to the manuscript during the composition process and who will pay for changes. Author's
alterations—always called AAs in the publishing and printing
trade—are any changes made by the author on composed type after
initial composition, except for those correcting errors made by compositors in setting type from manuscript; these are universally
called PEs. for printer's errors. Your contract with a compositor
should allow for some AAs without additional charges, and additional AAs at stated hourly—rather than per-page—charges. Note
that if you are allowed, for example, 10 percent of total initial composition costs for no-charge AAs, that does not mean that 10 percent
of the words in the manuscript can be altered on galleys without
additional charges, as alterations cost more per word or character
to do than initial composition. Rather, alterations will be charged
at the agreed-upon rate, with all charges under 10 percent of the
original cost being absorbed by the printer and the balance being
paid for by you, the author-publisher. As you read and correct galley
or page proofs, note which corrections are AAs and which PEs on
both the master set you return to the compositor and the copy you
keep. You may need that information later if you feel that you may
have been overcharged on AAs.

blueprints: The several kinds of blue, silver, brown, and other prints
are fully discussed in Chapter 5.

book face: Any typeface thought by a book's designer to be suitable
for a particular book may be described as a book face. Normally,
though, a printer, designer, or editor means by this a typeface that
has enough size and body to look good and be easy to read when
used in a book. Typewriter faces, for example, may look good on a
manuscript page because of their size and spacing but work very
badly when used in books because they are too large to use full
size and too thin and hard to read when reduced for book page use.
At the other extreme, some type faces used in newspapers may be
suitable for a fast scan or quick read but too small and dense for
use in books.

book size, trim size: A whole body of nomenclature, mostly archaic,
applies to book sizes, all based upon the way sheets coming off
presses of certain sizes were folded and the page sizes that resulted.

For modern American publishing purposes, it suffices to know that book size refers to the size of the trimmed pages of the book, rather than to the size of the covers of the book, and that sizes are described in inches. Hardcovers and trade paperbacks composed mainly of text normally run from about 5"x7" to 7"x10" in trimmed page size, while heavily illustrated books run in the 8½"x11" and 9"x12" range, with some running larger. Mass market paperbacks, and even some small hardcovers, go down into the 4¼"x7" range, with some novelty sizes going much smaller. Should anyone begin to discuss book sizes in terms of folios, quartos, octavos, and the like, ask that the discussion be carried on in modern terms.

bullets, boxes, fists, arrows, flags, and the rest: These are a whole body of typographical devices used to identify and accent elements within the main text, as when you run a list of comments that you want to set off, each indented and preceded by the heavy dot called a bullet; or when you box or otherwise set off a telling quote.

cast off: To cast off is to make an estimate of the number of printed pages that will result from your typed manuscript, taking different sets of composition assumptions. It is essentially designer's or printer's work, rather than something the self-publisher should attempt to do. If you do decide to try to make the estimate yourself, or are dealing with inexperienced people on the production side, then by all means set a few pages in the type size and style you have selected before making any final decision; then quite literally count the words on the pages set, and relate them to the average number of words on your manuscript pages. (Don't forget to count the sample manuscript pages in your final estimate.) Bear in mind that a difference of a single "point" in type size specifications can make a large difference in the number of pages in your finished book, as can the margins you use. Even two types of the same size may result in books of different size, as one type may be bulkier than the other, and therefore set fewer words on the same size line.

It is also wise to extend that kind of thinking to your choice of book paper. During the process of paper selection, be sure to make up a "dummy," composed of the number of sheets of paper that will result from your estimated number of pages. Only in that way can you be reasonably sure of the eventual bulk and weight of your book. And if you add a cover sample, and weigh the resulting blank book—with packing materials—you will also know approximately how much it will cost you to mail the book later on.

character, character count: A character is a single letter or space. It has become an increasingly important device as computer technology has moved into publishing and printing, as more and more cost estimates are stated in characters, rather than words or pages. For example, you may be quoted a composition price of $2.75 per thousand characters, and will need to relate that price to your manuscript. To do so roughly, you can take a fairly standard 250-word typed page, figure about five letters per word plus a space between each word and come up with 250 x6, or 1500 characters per page. But to relate that price to printed pages, which is the way printers normally quote per-page composition costs, you will need to make an estimate of the number of characters on the printed page of the book you are doing. Then the thing to do is to show the "per character" compositor sample pages, drawn from other books, and ask how much each page would cost to set; only in this way will you get proper comparison shopping composition estimates.

computer composition: Any way of setting type that uses a computer to perform the main typesetting function is properly described as computer composition; this includes everything from production of a floppy disc using a word processing program on a smallish home computer to the use of sophisticated—and very expensive—computers that can receive data from remote locations and use that data to directly drive high-speed composing machines as part of unified composition-to-printed-page systems that can go from first-draft writing to finished newspapers in a matter of hours. When you use a home computer to compose your book, you are using computer composition, even though in some instances your compositor may have to virtually re-keyboard your work to produce usable camera-ready copy.

co-op ad, advertising allowance: Publishers often share the cost of advertising with chain and independent booksellers. When such cost-sharing is done with specific ad placements, the resulting ads are called *co-op (for cooperative) ads*. When publisher cost-sharing is more general, as when it is expressed as a percentage of a bookseller's cost up to a fixed limit, or as a percentage of a bookseller's purchases from the publisher, the resulting arrangement is an *advertising allowance.* Small self-publishers should seriously consider such cost-sharing arrangements, especially locally and regionally, within budget considerations, as the bookseller who will spend some money to advertise your book is likely to place it well and sell it aggressively.

copyright: This is fully discussed in Chapter 4.

dirty copy, foul copy, penalty copy: These are discussed fully in Chapter 5.

discount: Not so long ago, two basic kinds of discounts were offered to their customers by publishers. The *long* discount was 40 percent off the list price (the price on the cover) of the book; the *short* discount was 20 percent off the list price. The long discount was offered on books offered primarily to booksellers for resale to consumers; the short discount was offered on books sold primarily to libraries and other institutions. For some rather complex reasons having to do with antitrust law, you could not—and still cannot—offer both discounts at the same time, which means that a decision to go with a short (20 percent) discount effectively guarantees that your book will not be routinely stocked by booksellers, who feel they cannot make enough profit to justify stocking the 20 percent discount book. Therefore, large and expensive reference books unlikely to be bought by most consumers are the only books likely to be sold at the 20 percent discount.

In recent years, with jobbers and chains increasingly influencing the bookselling scene, life has become somewhat more complicated for publishers—and more difficult. Books headed for libraries are still arranged much as they were, with library jobbers taking a little more than they used to, but not greatly affecting your margins from library sales. But bookseller sales are far less lucrative per unit, as chains are routinely demanding and getting 50 to 52 percent discounts, and jobbers are now beginning to do the same. Self-publishers also using distributors have to figure in distributors discounts, but this has been true all along. Returns of unsold books have also increased in recent years; the double shock of increased discounts and increased returns has made trade book publishing more difficult for all publishers.

elite, pica: These are the two most common typewriter type sizes. The *elite* type, which is the older form, runs about twelve characters to the inch horizontally, and has a smaller body than the *pica,* which runs about 10 characters to the inch horizontally, and is the standard modern typewriter type. Both are normally set on lines of the same height, so that lines typed singlespaced in elite type have space between lines, while those typed in pica type look as if they are placed quite solidly on the page, needing double-spacing to achieve comfortable readability. In trying to determine the number of words on a typed page, bear in mind that elite type is much smaller than pica; even though the number of lines on the page may be the same, far more words will be on the page using elite type.

first edition, limited edition: All the books run using the original plates of the work comprise the work's *first edition,* whether run all at once or in several printings. Later, if your book acquires collectible value, all the books in that first edition may be valuable, with the books run in the first printing the most valuable of the lot. For certain special works, you may also do a *limited edition,* which is usually a signed and numbered first printing, with limitation of the size of that printing aiming to increase the value of each of the volumes in the printing.

flush left, ragged right, justified, unjustified, proportionally spaced: These terms all refer to the handling of type margins on a page. Other than poetry, almost all type is set *flush left,* that is with an even left margin for all the lines in the text of a page. *Unjustified* lines are set *ragged right;* that means the margins on the right side of the page are uneven, as in most typescript. *Justified,* or *proportionally spaced,* lines have both left and right margins even on the page. What a proportionally spacing or justifying typewriter or computer does is to mechanically duplicate what typesetters have done since the invention of movable type, creating the even left and right margins we normally associate with books and other printed materials.

formats: These are fully discussed in Chapter 5.

front matter, preliminary matter, main text, back matter, end matter: These terms are fully discussed in Chapter 4 in the section subtitled The Elements of the Book. Note that *front matter* and *pre-*

liminary matter are synonyms, as are *back matter* and *end matter*. Also note that no particular order applies to the elements in all books, except that title, copyright, dedication, contents, foreword, preface, and introduction belong at the start, as front matter, while footnotes, which refer to text, must follow text, either in the main text or in back matter. As for the rest of the elements, placement in the work is a matter of choice. For example, the index, which usually appears at the back of the book, may for some large reference books, be placed much more usefully at the beginning of the book. And the wide ranges of textual materials, maps, tables, and illustrations generally described as appendixes may work best placed variously throughout the book, rather than in back matter.

ghostwriter: A writer who works with you by actually writing all or most of your book for you, while you receive sole credit for writing the book, is called a *ghostwriter.* Such a writer, receiving credit, becomes a *co-author.* An editor who works with you to write and rewrite your manuscript is neither, but rather a *developmental editor* or simply a good editor. In practice, there are times when the line between ghostwriter and developmental editor becomes rather fine.

graphics, art, illustrations: In practice, these terms are sometimes used quite interchangeably, although they have rather different meanings. *Graphics* describes all the non-word elements of the book—jacket, cover, page design and other format elements, original art, reproduced art, tables, charts, graphs, and whatever else is not straightforward text. *Art* refers to specific pieces of made-up work, such as illustrations and cover designs, ready to be made up with the text into camera-ready copy and then into plates for printing. *Illustrations* are pieces of visual material, such as line cuts, halftones, and color photos, that are placed into the book.

galleys: These are fully discussed in Chapter 5.

hardcover, hardbound, casebound, paperback, softcover, trade paperback, quality paperback, mass market paperback, looseleaf, comb, press: These can be some fairly confusing synonyms for overlapping publishing forms. *Hardcover, hardbound,* and *casebound* are all synonyms, describing hardcover books of all kinds, whatever their sizes or bindings, as long as contents are sewn or glued into bindings. *Paperback* and *softcover* are synonyms, describing books bound into any kind of soft cover, even though that cover may be made of very durable, flexible leather or plastic. *Trade paperback* and *quality paperback* are synonyms, describing higher priced and usually somewhat larger softcover books than are *mass market paperbacks*. The distinctions between trade and mass market paperbacks have been blurring over the years, however—the main distinction now being between the outlets through which they are marketed. *Looseleaf, comb,* and *press* are kinds of binders in which book contents are held by pressure or in drilled sets, rather than glued in.

heads, subheads, running heads: Heads are any legend topping sections of a work, such as chapter headings or chapter subsections. Some headings are subordinate to other headings; for example, when a chapter is broken up into sections and subsections, all but the chapter heading are called *subheads* and may be arranged in a hierarchy of subheads and sub-subheads. *Running heads* do not relate in the same way; they are the lines of copy on top (occasionally the bottom) of each page, identifying chapter titles and sometimes book titles or page or section contents.

image area: The *image area* is that portion of a page on which printing of any kind will appear, including any white space contained in that area. Usually it is all that space between the top of the running head at the top of the page and the last printed line of any kind on the page (whether text or page numbers), and between the furthest left and right printed lines or characters on the page. Where there are marginal notes or comments, they are part of the image area. Where illustrations *bleed* (that is, go to the trimmed edges of pages), the image area of these pages go to the ends of the illustrations. Note that often a seemingly small adjustment of margins can result in a considerably smaller or larger image area per page; this is one of the two main means of adjusting the number of pages in the finished book, the other being choice of type size.

in press, on press: In press means that a book is past manuscript and into the production process. *On press* is far more specific, meaning that your book is actually on a press and being run. Self-publishing press runs are usually rather modest, and a book that is on press is quite likely to be run in full once put on press, and then put through bindery and sent out to you rather quickly after that. But a book described to you as being "in press" may very well be stalled somewhere and in need of a push.

libel, slander, invasion of privacy: These are fully discussed in Chapter 4.

line cut, halftone, color separation: These are the three main kinds of illustration reproduction methods used in books, in order of expense. The *line cut,* a synonym for *line engraving,* is an engraving on a plate (or a reproduction of an engraving), which is then photographically reproduced, as composed text copy is reproduced; this often works quite well visually on the kind of book paper used for text. A *halftone* is a reproduction of a photograph or other image, which must be done through a special screen and results in a dot pattern which can be used to reproduce the original; it usually works better on glossy stock than on normal book paper. The *color separation* should really be called a color reproduction, as a "separation" refers to a reproducing technique now being superseded by new technology. Color reproductions require glossy stock to work well and are also more expensive to do; if you intend to use some in your book, be keenly aware of their probable high cost and get firm estimates based on samples of the kinds of illustrations you will use before deciding to go ahead.

makeready: This is the process of putting a piece of work on a printing press and preparing it to be run. *Makeready time*—the time it takes to do this—is a very important element of cost for self-publishers, many of whom do short press runs, in which makeready time is a large part of total press time and therefore of book manufacturing cost. When comparison shopping costs, bear in mind that one press will suit your needs far better than another and that the printers you are talking with will quite naturally try to sell you their services, even though their equipment may not really be right for the job. For example, a wonderfully fast press that is fine for long runs may not be at all good for short runs, because it requires so much time to make ready for printing. Note that those printers who make short runs a substantial part of their business are most likely to have equipment that suits self-publisher's needs.

out of print, out of stock, back ordered: When you have gone temporarily *out of stock* on your book, you plan to reprint. In that situation, orders coming in are *back ordered,* to be fulfilled when you have books again. For in the book trade, a book that is *out of print* is one that its publisher does not currently plan to reprint; orders placed for such a book will then be canceled, and booksellers would inform retail customers that the book is no longer available. If you are temporarily unable to fill orders but are planning to reprint, be sure you inform those who order that you are out of stock rather than out of print.

perfect bound: Perfect binding, which is a very far from perfect way of binding books, is discussed fully in Chapter 5.

permissions: These are fully discussed in Chapter 4.

presses: There are several good ways of getting ink on paper, and most printers are justifiably proud of their equipment, which has roughly the same place in their scheme of things as your books have in yours. One printer may have a wonderful *web-fed rotary press,* meaning a press that spins around as it prints, fed by a continuous roll of paper, and works very fast—though it may take a comparatively long time to set up. Another may have a *rotary press* that is sheet-fed (that is, fed by a pile of sheets), works somewhat slower, and takes less time to set up. Another may have a *sheet-fed, flat-bed press,* the other main job shop press in use today, which is just right for you in makeready time and speed, but of not quite the right size for your book, so that you waste a lot of paper in printing. Another may be enormously proud of having acquired a *jet press,* which—like most high-speed computer printers—sprays ink on paper as it goes by, works tremendously fast, and may be wholly inappropriate for your publishing needs because of its high set-up costs. Your concern as a publisher is to get the most efficient organization and presses you can find working to produce your books cost effectively. You are unlikely to go far wrong if you limit your inquiries and comparison shopping to experienced short-run book printers.

pre-publication: This is fully discussed in Chapter 5.

proofs: The several kinds of *proofs* are fully discussed in Chapter 5.

rights: The several kinds of *rights* are fully discussed in Chapter 6.

saddle sewing, Smythe sewing, sidestitching: These and other binding methods are fully discussed in Chapter 5.

selection, main selection, alternate selection, co-selection, dividend: A *selection* is a book club purchase of multiple copies of your book or the right to print their own edition of your book. A *main selection* is that book the club will send its members without their asking for it, unless their members exercise their right to turn down the book within a specified period (which is called the exercise of a negative option). An *alternate selection* is a book that members may choose instead of, or as well as, the main selection. A *co-selection* means that your book is teamed up with another book, the two sold together to members as a single selection. A *dividend* is the use of your book as an inducement or premium, as when copies can be purchased by prospective members for one dollar when they join the book club, or when it is supplied free or at very low cost to all those current members who have purchased a certain number of books.

self-publishing, vanity publishing: These are fully discussed in Chapter 1.

serif, sans serif: Beware the book designer or compositor who suggests that you set your book in a lovely, modern sans serif type. *Serifs* are small projections off the ends of letters, added to give more body to the typeface; most classic and widely used bookfaces have them. Typefaces characterized by the presence of serifs also vary the thicknesses of the body of the type. *Sans serif* means without a serif; typefaces without serifs also tend to have no variation in body thicknesses, instead having letters of uniform thicknesses. Sans serif typefaces are widely used for some kinds of periodicals; they are much less successful as book typefaces, as most tend to develop pages that are monotonous and therefore hard to read.

signatures: These are fully discussed in Chapter 5.

trade book: A *trade book* is a book that is sold through trade outlets, which are bookstores and other outlets selling directly to consumers. Such a book may also be sold by mail and to libraries and other institutions; the identification as a trade book stems more from the kind of discount offered and the selling price than from the content of the book. Nor are the distinctions between the kinds of books terribly clear; a book of reference selling at $40 but carrying a 40 percent discount will be described by some in the publishing and bookselling trades as a reference book and by others as a trade book. If you wish to try to sell your book through trade outlets, offer the trade discount, accept returns for full credit, and describe your book as a trade book, whatever its content and however else you sell it.

type sizes, point system: These are discussed fully in Chapter 5.

video display terminal (VDT): This is the ubiquitous computer "terminal," increasingly an integral part of modern life. In publishing and printing, as in all other uses, it has about as many names as it has programmed functions. When used for receiving information, for example, it may be called a videotext terminal; it may be programmed for publication design, general word processing, or editing, in each case being labeled by function, as when a VDT is called an editing terminal. Eventually every home will have one.

Index

MENTOR and SIGNET Reference Books

(0451)

- [ ] **ALL ABOUT WORDS by Maxwell Numberg and Morris Rosenblum.** Two language experts call on history, folklore, and anecdotes to explain the origin, development, and meaning of words. (620712—$3.50)

- [ ] **WORDS FROM THE MYTHS by Isaac Asimov.** A fascinating exploration of our living heritage from the ancient world. Isaac Asimov retells the ancient stories—from Chaos to the siege of Troy—and describes their influence on modern language . . . and modern life. (123778)—$1.95)

- [ ] **INSTANT WORD POWER by Norman Lewis.** A fast, effective way to build a rich and dynamic vocabulary. Entertaining exercises and challenging self-tests enable the student to master hundreds of new words and polish spelling and grammar skills. (117913—$3.50)*

- [ ] **MASTERING SPEED READING by Norman C. Maberly.** Basic steps and drills with illustrations, charts and tests provide self-instruction in speed reading. (136969—$2.50)

- [ ] **A DICTIONARY OF DIFFICULT WORDS by Robert H. Hill.** The essential companion to every abridged dictionary complete with 15,000 entries on business, technology, culture, medicine, science, acronyms, and foreign words. (118030—$3.95)

- [ ] **THE NEW AMERICAN WEBSTER HANDY COLLEGE DICTIONARY.** Over 100,000 definitions in this comprehensive dictionary which includes illustrations, abbreviations, geographical names and colloquialisms. (125371—$2.50)*

- [ ] **THE NEW AMERICAN ROGET'S COLLEGE THESAURUS in Dictionary Form.** Revised edition. Synonyms and antonyms in an alphabetical listing. Easy to use. A must for every library. (125398—$2.95)*

*Prices slightly higher in Canada

Buy them at your local bookstore or use this convenient coupon for ordering.

NEW AMERICAN LIBRARY
P.O. Box 999, Bergenfield, New Jersey 07621

Please send me the books I have checked above. I am enclosing $_____(please add $1.00 to this order to cover postage and handling). Send check or money order—no cash or C.O.D.'s. Prices and numbers are subject to change without notice.

Name_____

Address_____

City_____State_____Zip Code_____

Allow 4-6 weeks for delivery.
This offer is subject to withdrawal without notice.

Ⓟ

More from PLUME

To order, use the convenient coupon on next page.